ROSE ELLIOT
THE
CLASSIC
VEGETARIAN
COOKBOOK

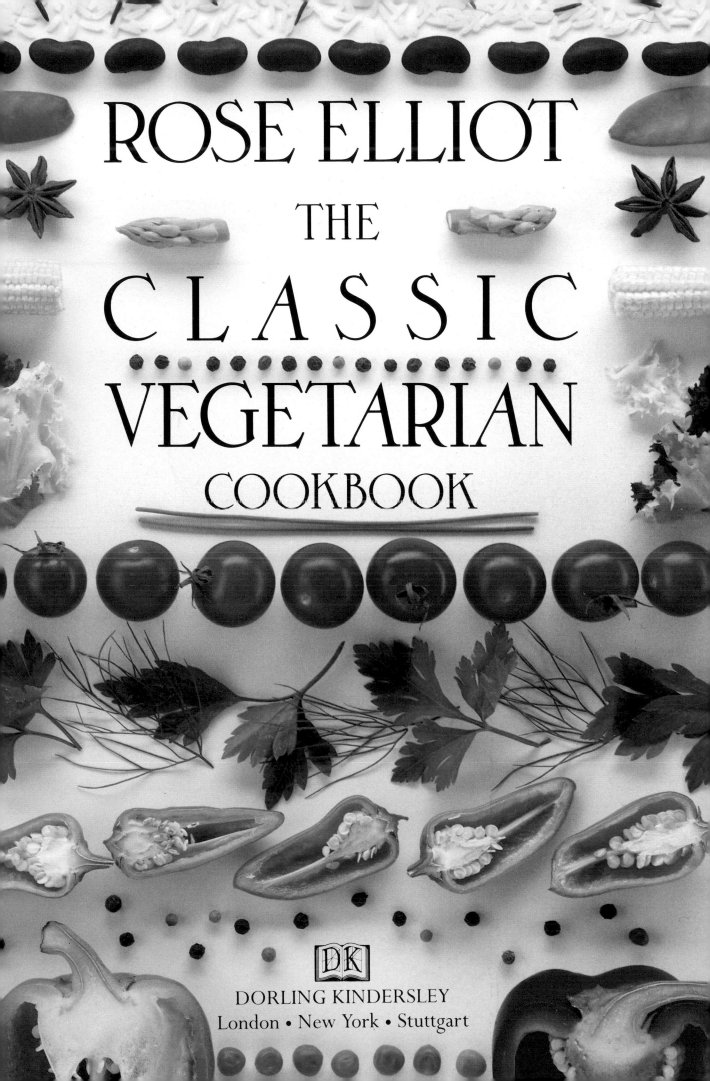

ROSE ELLIOT

THE

CLASSIC

VEGETARIAN

COOKBOOK

DK

DORLING KINDERSLEY

London • New York • Stuttgart

A DORLING KINDERSLEY BOOK

Project Editor
Mari Roberts

Art Editor
Tracey Clarke

Designer
Kate Scott

Managing Editor
Rosie Pearson

Managing Art Editor
Carole Ash

Photography
Clive Streeter
Amanda Heywood

Senior Production Manager
Maryann Rogers

*To vegetarians, and would-be vegetarians,
with love*

First published in Great Britain in 1994
by Dorling Kindersley Limited,
9 Henrietta Street, London WC2E 8PS

Reprinted 1994

A CIP catalogue record for this book is available
from the British Library.

ISBN 0 7513 0066 7

Reproduced in Thailand by
J. Film Process Co., Ltd.

Printed and bound in Italy by A. Mondadori, Verona

CONTENTS

INTRODUCTION 6

CLASSIC DISHES

*A unique photographic catalogue featuring
ten key classic vegetarian dishes
with ingredients and recipe variations*

INTRODUCTION

When I was about three I first made the connection between the fish that my mother was preparing for supper and the fish that swim in the sea. I made a fuss, which I can still remember, and refused to eat my meal. That is when I became vegetarian.

Another trait that surfaced early was a love of cooking. My mother tells stories of my early experiments in the kitchen as a child, when my use of ingredients was lavish, and the piles of washing up immense. My parents' tolerance paid off. They ran a retreat centre, and the skills that I acquired enabled me to take over the cooking there when I was in my late teens. There were few vegetarian recipes to guide me, so I frequently experimented. Guests constantly asked for my recipes and so, audaciously and rather innocently at such a young age, I wrote my first cookery book, *Simply Delicious*, which was published in 1967. This was one of the first exclusively vegetarian cookbooks published in the UK and its success led to more – in fact, I didn't stop writing and have now produced over forty books.

Over the years my style of cooking, although always vegetarian, has changed and developed greatly, as an ever-increasing range of ingredients has become available and as I've travelled, learned and continued to experiment. The emphasis on straightforward dishes that are fairly quick and undemanding to make has, however, remained. This is partly because of my circumstances – with home, family and career to manage – and partly because simple fresh food, with all the flavour of the natural ingredients intact, is my preference.

The many recipes I have selected and created for this book fall into two main categories: long-established, traditional recipes and innovative new ones. You will find the best of classic vegetarian cuisine here, such as delectable fondue, creamy gratin dauphinois and colourful, crunchy salads, together with fresh ideas for vegetable terrines and roulades, delicate crêpes and melting pastries. Even though desserts need not be designated "vegetarian", I don't believe a cookbook is complete without them, and so here you will find recipes ranging from chocolate brownies to a rose-petal sorbet.

I have given suggestions for creating meals from these recipes in the menu planning section, and you will find they cover most occasions, from casual, loosely structured suppers to formal dinners. Whether you are fully vegetarian or demi-vegetarian, or simply want to make delicious meals for vegetarian friends and family, I hope that you will take pleasure in reading this book, using the recipes and enjoying the results.

Rose Elliot

CLASSIC DISHES

*The ten classic dishes featured here represent
the best of the world's vegetarian cuisine. From
a light savoury strudel to a Thai-style stir-fry, a
vegetable terrine to a golden cheese soufflé,
these dishes and their variations provide a taster
for the recipes to come later in the book,
and an overview of how exciting
vegetarian cookery can be.*

TERRINES

Colourful and eye-catching, vegetable terrines are a modern vegetarian classic. They are simple to make, delicious and versatile. A terrine may be served as a starter or as a light main course, and many are good hot or cold. This beautiful, fragrant terrine is perfect for a celebratory summer meal; it serves 6 as a starter.

TOMATO, COURGETTE, RED PEPPER & BASIL

INGREDIENTS

butter and dry grated Parmesan to coat the tin
15ml (1 tbsp) olive oil
1 medium-sized onion, chopped
1 clove garlic, chopped
400g (14oz) can whole peeled tomatoes,
coarsely chopped, with juice
300g (10oz) courgettes, cut into 3mm (⅛in) slices
1 large red pepper, quartered
45ml (3 tbsps) single cream
2 tbsps freshly grated Parmesan cheese
1 tbsp tomato purée, preferably sundried
3 free-range eggs, beaten
salt and freshly ground black pepper
bunch of fresh basil, including some sprigs to garnish

PREPARATION

1 Preheat the oven to 160°C/325°F/gas 3. Line a 500g (1lb) loaf tin with nonstick paper, grease lightly with butter and dust with dry Parmesan.
2 Warm the oil in a saucepan over a moderate heat, add the onion, cover and cook for 5 minutes. Add the garlic and cook for another minute.
3 Pour in the tomatoes together with their juice. Reduce the heat and simmer, uncovered, until the liquid has evaporated and the mixture reduced: about 15 minutes. Remove from the heat.
4 Boil the courgettes until tender, drain, refresh under cold water and pat dry with kitchen paper.
5 Grill and peel the pepper as shown on page 144. Remove the stalk and seeds, and cut into strips.
6 Into the tomato mixture stir the cream, Parmesan, tomato purée and eggs. Season well.
7 Fill the tin in layers: some tomato mixture, the courgettes, more tomato, the basil leaves, and the the strips of red pepper with the last of the tomato.
8 Bake the terrine in a bain-marie (see page 147) in the preheated oven until set and firm: about 1¼ hours. Allow to cool before turning out.

Red pepper

Courgettes

Canned tomatoes

Garlic

Onion

Olive oil

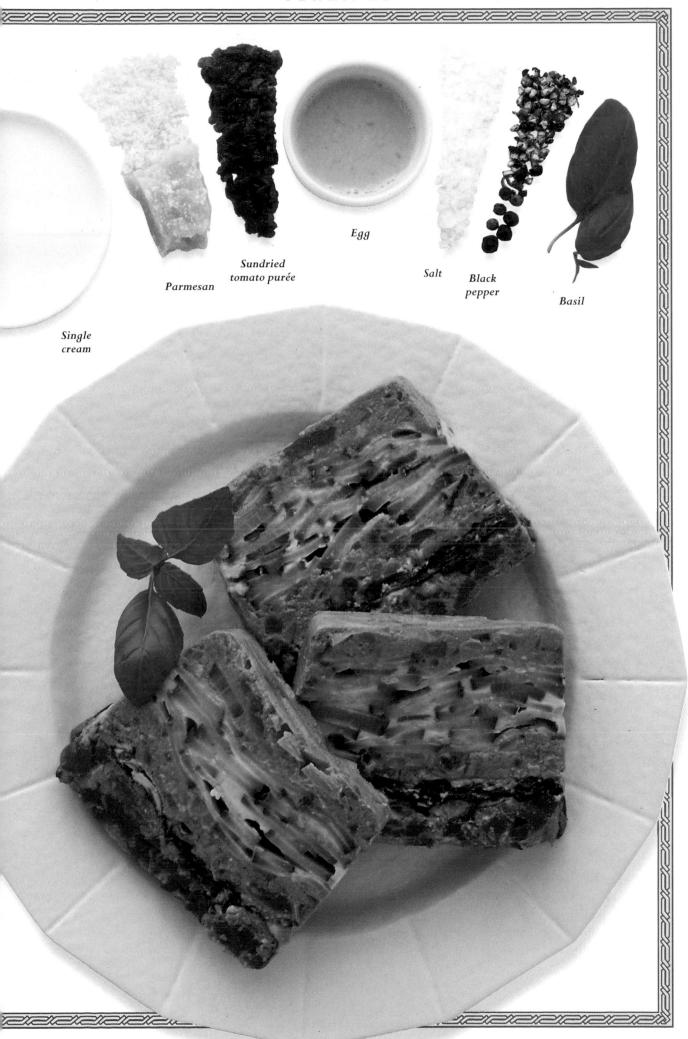

Single
cream

Parmesan

Sundried
tomato purée

Egg

Salt

Black
pepper

Basil

A SELECTION OF TERRINES

VEGETABLES IN A SPINACH COAT

Layers of rich-tasting artichoke heart, asparagus and sundried tomato are set in a curd cheese and chives mixture and wrapped in spinach leaves. The sauce is made from sundried tomatoes (page 121).

See page 67 for recipe.

PUMPKIN, BROCCOLI & LEEK

This is a good terrine for autumn or winter, making the most of the colours of puréed and sliced pumpkin, which contrast with the broccoli and leek. Green pepper sauce (page 120), shown here, is an excellent accompaniment, as is mayonnaise mixed with Greek yogurt. Garnish with chervil.

See page 69 for recipe.

STRIPED VEGETABLE

Bright stripes of carrot, broad bean and turnip, layered with chervil, make this a stunning opening to a meal, and fresh tomato sauce (page 121) is a dramatic addition. You can use other vegetables in the terrine according to the season, aiming for contrasting colours and tastes.

See page 68 for recipe.

PEPPERS & BABY SWEETCORN

Mediterranean flavours and bright colours make this a favourite summer terrine for the first course of a light salad meal. A thin pesto sauce (page 123) and a basil garnish set it off well, in both colour and flavour.

See page 66 for recipe.

GREEN PEA, MINT & CAULIFLOWER

This is a refreshing, summery dish, perfect with Greek yogurt brightened up by a little saffron, as here, or with a warm hollandaise sauce (page 123). The clean taste of the mint is complemented by the sweetness of the peas and the mildness of the cauliflower.

See page 67 for recipe.

LENTIL, CARROT & FENNEL

A light lentil mixture flavoured with turmeric and mixed with carrot, fennel and flat-leaf parsley makes this unusual terrine. It is delicious cold, either as a starter or as part of a buffet. Here it is served with red pepper sauce (page 120) and garnished with dill.

See page 68 for recipe.

OMELETTES

A classic omelette – folded, and slightly runny inside – is quick and easy to make, and delicious at any time of the day. The technique is simple, and success depends largely on having a frying pan of the right size: if it is too big for the number of eggs, the omelette will be thin and tough; if too small, it will be spongy and thick. Omelettes are versatile, too. You can fill them with a wide choice of ingredients, such as mushrooms, ratatouille, or for a particular treat, shavings of black truffle. This is a two-egg omelette, ideal for one person, cooked in a 15cm (6in) frying pan, with the simple addition of fragrant chopped fresh herbs stirred into the eggs before they are cooked.

Free-range egg

Salt

Black pepper

Flat-leaf parsley

FRESH HERB OMELETTE

INGREDIENTS

2 free-range eggs
salt and freshly ground black pepper
2 tsps finely chopped fresh flat-leaf parsley
1 tsp finely chopped fresh chives
1 tsp finely chopped fresh chervil
1 tsp finely chopped fresh tarragon
15g (½oz) butter

PREPARATION

1 Break the eggs into a bowl and beat them lightly until the whites and yolks have just combined. Season with salt and black pepper. Add the herbs.
2 Place a small frying pan (15cm/6in across the base) over a moderate heat and, when it is hot, put in the butter, turn the heat up to high, and swirl the butter around the pan without letting it brown.
3 Pour in the eggs, tipping the pan so that it is evenly coated. Using a fork, gently draw the edges of the egg towards the centre and let the liquid egg run to the edges. Keep doing this until the omelette is almost set but still a little moist on top – it takes around a minute.
4 To serve the omelette folded in half as shown here, hold the pan over a warmed plate and slide the omelette on to the plate, allowing the top half to flip over and cover the bottom half on the plate. Alternatively, fold it in three. While the omelette is still in the pan, flip one third over towards the centre, then slide it on to a warmed plate, unfolded edge first, allowing the folded part to flip over and cover the rest. (See page 148 for an illustration of this method.)
5 Serve and eat at once.

Chives

Chervil

Tarragon

Butter

FILO PIES & PARCELS

Crisp and golden filo parcels and strudels, filled with moist and tender vegetables, are delicious and surprisingly easy to make. Thin sheets of ready-made filo pastry can be used for elaborate main dishes, such as the sliced strudel shown here, or for simple but original snacks (see overleaf). Ingredients may be varied to suit the occasion. For example, make the vegetable strudel with parsnips and blue cheese instead of the Swiss chard, and use pinenuts instead of olives. This strudel serves 6.

VEGETABLE STRUDEL

INGREDIENTS

500g (1lb) Swiss chard, leaves and stems separated
and roughly torn
250g (8oz) carrots, cut into sticks
250g (8oz) cooked artichoke bases (page 146), sliced
2 free-range egg yolks
150ml (5fl oz) single cream
2 tbsps finely chopped fresh flat-leaf parsley
salt and freshly ground black pepper
1 packet of filo pastry and melted butter for brushing
60g (2oz) black olives, pitted and sliced

PREPARATION

1 Preheat the oven to 200°C/400°F/gas 6.
2 Cook the Swiss chard leaves until tender in just the water that clings to them after washing. Cook the Swiss chard stems and the carrots separately in a little boiling water until tender. Drain.
3 Put the vegetables into a big bowl with the artichoke, egg yolks, cream and parsley. Combine well. Season to taste with salt and black pepper.
4 Spread a clean tea towel on the work surface and place on it two or four sheets of filo pastry (depending on their size), side by side, over-lapping by 1cm (½in) to make a rectangle about 50 x 45cm (20 x 18in). Brush all over with melted butter. Make another rectangle of the same size on top of the first and brush with butter again.
5 Spread the filling evenly over the filo to within 2.5cm (1in) of the edges. Sprinkle the olives on top. Turn over the edges to make a "hem", then roll up the strudel firmly from one of the long edges. Brush it all over with melted butter. For extra flakiness, wrap one or two more sheets of filo around the strudel, brushing with butter.
6 Place the strudel on a baking sheet, curving it into a half moon. Bake until crisp and golden brown: about 35 minutes. Serve at once, or recrisp later by returning it briefly to a hot oven.

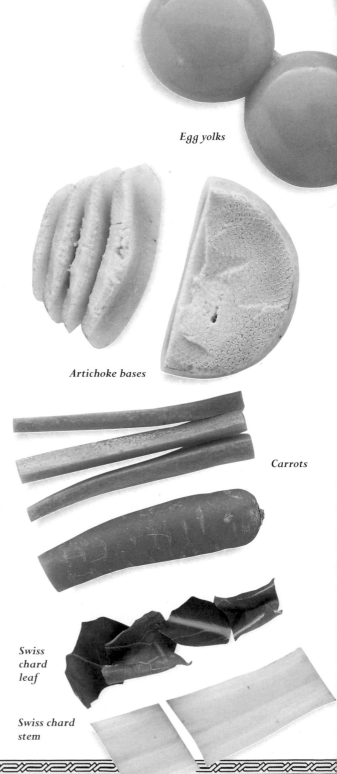

Egg yolks

Artichoke bases

Carrots

Swiss chard leaf

Swiss chard stem

Single cream

Flat-leaf parsley

Salt

Black pepper

Filo pastry brushed with butter

Olives

FILO SHAPES & PARCELS

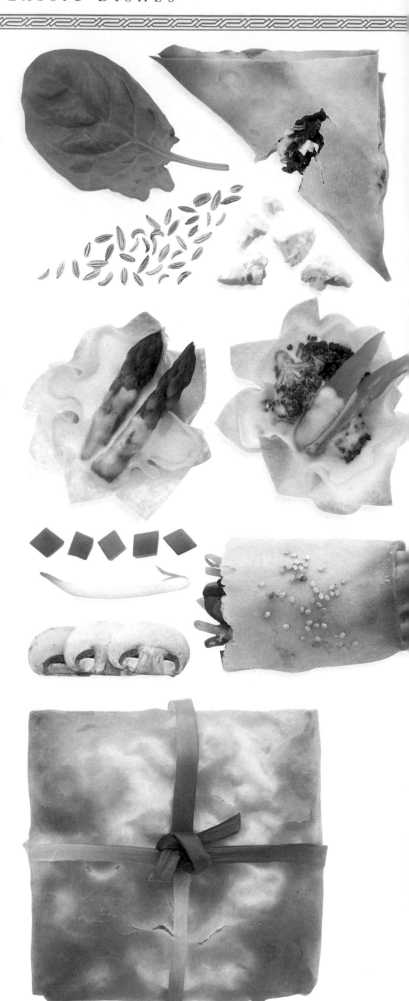

LITTLE GREEK PIES

Bite-size versions of a classic Greek pie, these crisp triangles contain a mixture of salty feta cheese, spinach enlivened by fennel seeds, and a little onion. They make an excellent snack, hot or cold.

See page 110 for recipe.

FILO FLOWERS

Small squares of filo pastry arranged into flower shapes make pretty containers for mouthwatering asparagus with hollandaise sauce. Other vegetables work well too, such as broccoli with strips of tomato. The flowers can be made in advance, but fill them at the last minute so they stay crisp.

See page 109 for recipe.

SPRING ROLLS

Filo is perfect for spring rolls, which can be deep-fried or, as here, brushed with oil, sprinkled with sesame seeds and baked. The filling is a Chinese-style mixture of peppers, beansprouts and mushrooms.

See page 109 for recipe.

LEEK PARCELS

These light filo parcels are filled with a creamy leek mixture. To hint at the filling, serve the parcels "tied up" with a leek ribbon. Tying up is easier if the raw leek is first dipped in hot water to soften it.

See page 109 for recipe.

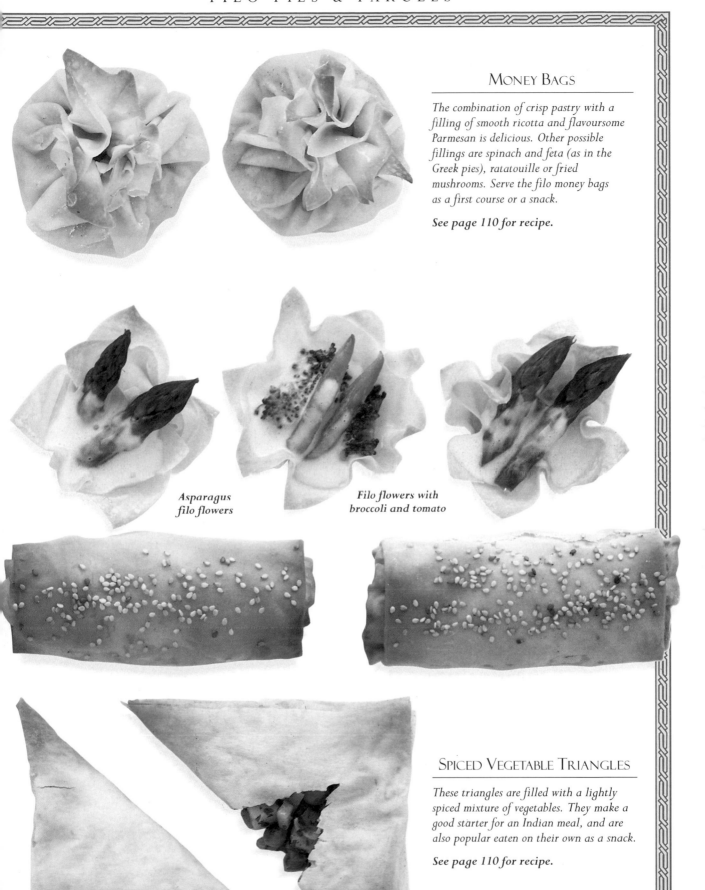

MONEY BAGS

The combination of crisp pastry with a filling of smooth ricotta and flavoursome Parmesan is delicious. Other possible fillings are spinach and feta (as in the Greek pies), ratatouille or fried mushrooms. Serve the filo money bags as a first course or a snack.

See page 110 for recipe.

Asparagus filo flowers

Filo flowers with broccoli and tomato

SPICED VEGETABLE TRIANGLES

These triangles are filled with a lightly spiced mixture of vegetables. They make a good starter for an Indian meal, and are also popular eaten on their own as a snack.

See page 110 for recipe.

PASTA

Springtime pasta, or pasta primavera, is a classic Italian dish, full of fresh spring vegetables and herbs. You can use any tender young vegetables: courgettes, asparagus and baby carrots are delicious options. The trick with pasta is to bite a piece as it boils to ensure you don't pass the stage known to Italians as *al dente*, where the pasta still offers some resistance to the teeth. Pasta primavera serves 4 as a first course, 2 as a main course.

PASTA PRIMAVERA

INGREDIENTS

175g (6oz) fresh podded or frozen broad beans
30g (1oz) butter
125g (4oz) green beans, trimmed
125g (4oz) mangetout, trimmed
250g (8oz) pasta ribbons, such as fettuccine or linguine
2 tbsps chopped fresh flat-leaf parsley
1 tbsp chopped fresh dill
1 tbsp chopped fresh chives
salt and freshly ground black pepper

PREPARATION

1 Cook the broad beans in a little boiling water until just tender: about 2 minutes. Drain, allow to cool, then pop out of their skins using your finger and thumb. Put them into a medium-sized saucepan along with the butter and set aside.
2 Pour 2 litres (3½ pints) of water into a large pan and place over a high heat. This is for the pasta.
3 Put the green beans in a small pan, cover with boiling water and cook until tender: 3–4 minutes. Drain and add to the pan with the broad beans.
4 Put the mangetout in the small pan, cover with boiling water and cook for 1 minute. Drain and add to the other vegetables. Place over a gentle heat and warm the vegetables in the butter.
5 When the water for the pasta reaches a rolling boil, drop the pasta in. Allow the water to come back to the boil, give the pasta a quick stir, then let the water boil steadily until the pasta is tender but still offers some resistance to the teeth: bite a piece to find out. Pasta cooks in a few minutes.
6 Drain the pasta but leave some water clinging to it, and put it back into the hot pan. Add the warm vegetables with their butter, and the herbs. Toss well, season to taste with salt and black pepper, and toss again, making sure the pasta is well coated. Serve at once.

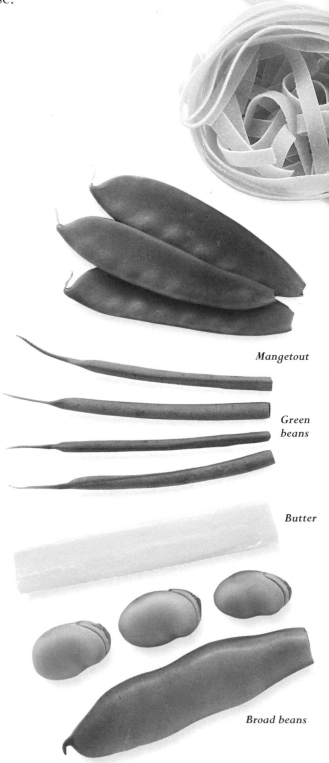

Mangetout

Green beans

Butter

Broad beans

Flat-leaf
parsley

Dill

Chives

Salt

Black
pepper

Fettuccine

STUFFED VEGETABLES

Many vegetables lend themselves to being filled, and the ingredients you can use are varied and versatile. Stuffed vegetables make compact, tasty snacks for a picnic, and can grace a dinner table, too. Artichokes, in particular, make a stunning first course. This recipe serves 4 as a starter, with an artichoke per person.

TOMATO-FILLED ARTICHOKES

INGREDIENTS

4 large globe artichokes, stalks and leaf points removed
½ lemon
THE FILLING
15ml (1 tbsp) olive oil
1 small onion, chopped
1 clove garlic, chopped
400g (14oz) can whole peeled tomatoes,
coarsely chopped, with juice
salt and freshly ground black pepper
8 fresh basil leaves, roughly torn
fresh chives, to garnish

PREPARATION

1 Make sure the bases of the prepared artichokes are level, then rub all the cut surfaces with the lemon to preserve the colour. Fill a saucepan large enough to hold the artichokes (or two that will each hold two) with water and bring to the boil.
2 Put the artichokes into the boiling water and cover with a small plate to keep them submerged. Let them simmer for about 30 minutes or until you can easily pull a leaf from one of them. Drain them upside down in a colander or on a wire rack.
3 Preheat the oven to 180°C/350°F/gas 4.
4 Make the filling. Warm the oil in a saucepan over a moderate heat, add the onion, cover and cook for 5 minutes. Add the garlic and cook for another 1–2 minutes. Pour in the tomatoes with their juice and cook, uncovered, until the mixture has reduced: about 15 minutes. Remove from the heat, season to taste and add the basil.
5 Take the artichokes and pull out the pale inner leaves, then use a teaspoon to scoop out the fluffy choke. Spoon the tomato filling into the hollow that is left. Place in a shallow casserole dish, cover with foil and bake in the preheated oven until heated through: about 20 minutes.
6 Serve on warmed plates with chopped chives sprinkled on top. To eat, tear off the leaves one by one and dip the fleshy, edible part in the filling. Work your way down to the base, and eat that too.

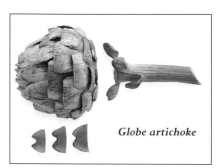

Globe artichoke

Lemon

Olive oil

Onion

Garlic

Canned tomatoes

Salt

Black
pepper

Basil

Chives

STUFFED VEGETABLES

CHILLI LIME AVOCADOS

These avocados are stuffed with a mixture of onion, garlic, chilli, chives and lime, and baked just long enough to heat through — if they are cooked for longer, their flavour is spoilt. Garnish with slices of lime and any fresh herb that is available; here it is coriander.

See page 63 for recipe.

BABY AUBERGINES WITH MUSHROOMS & NUTS

Tomatoes and parsley are combined with mushrooms and pinenuts to make the stuffing for these attractive baby aubergines. You can use larger aubergines if the baby ones are unavailable, or if you lack the time to prepare the more fiddly smaller ones. Stuffed aubergines are delicious both hot — or warm — and cold.

See page 64 for recipe.

PEPPERS WITH GRILLED VEGETABLES

This is an eye-catching way to serve grilled vegetables — and easy to do because you grill the peppers and all the vegetables together. Basil is used here to garnish.

See page 65 for recipe.

HERBY TOMATOES

Thyme combined with breadcrumbs, olive oil and flat-leaf parsley (which can also be a garnish) makes a fragrant stuffing for a large tomato. This is an ideal summer dish when tomatoes and herbs are plentiful and at their best. The flavour always transports me straight to Provence.

See page 65 for recipe.

CREAM CHEESE MUSHROOMS

For a simple yet flavoursome stuffing for mushrooms use cream cheese with herbs and garlic. Small or large mushrooms may be used but they should be as open and flat as possible. Lemon strips (page 145) and dill make a delicate garnish.

See page 65 for recipe.

COURGETTES WITH ALMONDS & RED PEPPER

This is a particularly good mix of flavours, colours and textures. Yellow peppers may be used instead of red, and pinenuts or pistachios instead of almonds. Fresh thyme is added to the filling, and here thyme is also the garnish.

See page 63 for recipe.

SOUFFLES

Served the instant it comes out of the oven, a soufflé is one of the most impressive dishes you can make. The timing is crucial but the preparation is easy, and much can be done in advance. It is important to use the right-sized soufflé dish so that when the mixture expands it does not overflow on to the oven floor. This delicious, golden soufflé, garnished with edible flowers, serves 3 people as a generous main course.

Parmesan

Egg yolks

Milk

Plain flour

Butter

FOUR-CHEESE SOUFFLE

INGREDIENTS

30g (1oz) butter, plus extra to grease the dish
30g (1oz) plain flour
300ml (½ pint) milk
5 free-range eggs, separated (with 1 yolk unused)
45g (1½oz) Parmesan cheese, grated
45g (1½oz) Gruyère cheese, grated
30g (1oz) blue cheese, crumbled
30g (1oz) mozzarella cheese, diced
salt and freshly ground black pepper
edible flowers such as nasturtiums, to garnish

PREPARATION

1 Melt the butter and stir in the flour, then slowly add the milk to make a béchamel sauce, as shown on page 148. Leave it to simmer over a very gentle heat for 10 minutes, then allow to cool slightly.
2 Stir four of the egg yolks (save the fifth to use in another recipe) and all the cheeses into the sauce and season to taste. Transfer to a bowl.

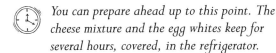

You can prepare ahead up to this point. The cheese mixture and the egg whites keep for several hours, covered, in the refrigerator.

3 Preheat the oven to 200°C/400°F/gas 6. Butter a 1.5-litre (2½-pint) soufflé dish and tie a piece of buttered nonstick paper around the outside extending at least 5cm (2in) above the rim.
4 In a greasefree bowl, whisk the five egg whites until they are stiff but not so dry that you can slice them. Stir 2 tablespoons of egg white into the soufflé mixture to loosen it, then gently fold in the rest of the egg white using a metal spoon.
5 Pour the mixture into the dish. To make the soufflé rise in a top-hat shape, draw the handle of a wooden spoon through its surface in a circle.
6 Bake until the soufflé is risen and golden brown: about 25 minutes. Serve immediately.

Gruyère

Blue cheese

Mozzarella

Salt

Black pepper

Egg white

Nasturtium

FLANS & TARTS

My way of cooking a classic savoury flan is to "waterproof" the pastry case with hot oil and to pre-cook the custard. The result is a crisp case with a light filling. This recipe makes four individual flans, each with tender broccoli and creamy Brie in a light savoury custard.

BROCCOLI & BRIE FLANS

INGREDIENTS

THE PASTRY

4 x 10cm (4in) shortcrust pastry cases
(pages 150−1), uncooked
30ml (2 tbsps) olive oil
1 shallot, chopped
1 clove garlic, chopped

THE FILLING

125g (4oz) broccoli florets
1 free-range egg
150ml (5fl oz) single cream
salt and freshly ground black pepper
freshly grated nutmeg
60g (2oz) Brie, thinly sliced
2 tbsps freshly grated Parmesan cheese
1−2 tbsps pinenuts

PREPARATION

1 Preheat the oven to 200°C/400°F/gas 6.
2 Prepare and bake the pastry cases as described on pages 150−1. About 5 minutes before they are done, heat the oil in a saucepan and fry the shallot and garlic until golden. As soon as the cases come out of the oven, pour the hot oil into them, letting it run over the pastry to waterproof and flavour it.
3 Turn the oven down to 160°C/325°F/gas 3.
4 Half-boil, half-steam the broccoli in a little water until barely tender: 3−4 minutes. Drain, refresh with cold running water and leave to dry in a colander.
5 To make the custard, break the egg into a small bowl, pour in the cream and mix well. Pour the mixture into a saucepan and stir over a gentle heat until it begins to coat the back of the spoon. Take off the heat, season with salt, black pepper and nutmeg, and stir in half the Parmesan.
6 Arrange the Brie and the broccoli in the base of each flan and pour the custard over them. Sprinkle the rest of the Parmesan and the pinenuts on top. Bake until the filling is set and golden brown: 20−25 minutes. Serve hot, warm or cold.

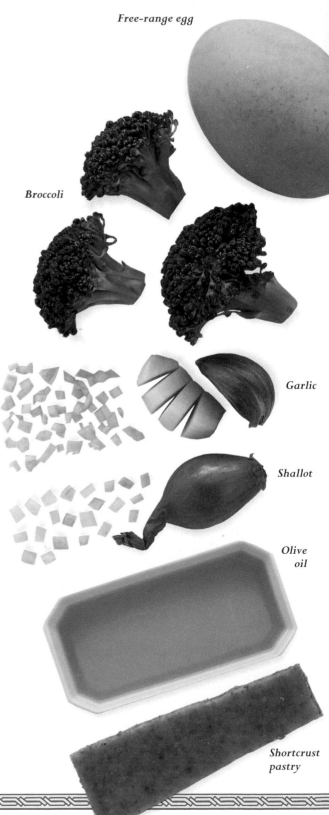

Free-range egg

Broccoli

Garlic

Shallot

Olive oil

Shortcrust pastry

Salt

Black
pepper

Nutmeg

Brie

Parmesan

Single cream

Pinenuts

TINY FLANS & TARTLETS

CHERRY TOMATO BARQUETTES

In these boat-shaped tartlets, cherry tomatoes are baked in a light custard. The cases may be pre-baked or not, as you prefer, but ensure the pastry is thin.

See page 105 for recipe.

Black olive and tomato   **Feta, rocket and sundried tomato**

LEEK & SESAME FLAN

The mixture of creamy leeks with sesame seed pastry is unusual and delicious. The pastry case should be pre-baked and "waterproofed" with hot oil as described on page 151 to make it beautifully crisp.

See page 105 for recipe.

TINY FLANS

Mini versions of flans can be filled with unusual ingredients for originality. Small avocado and spring onion flans are complemented well by fragrant carrot and cardamom ones, and together they are excellent as part of a party spread.

See page 105 for recipe.

Avocado and spring onion   **Carrot and cardamom**

MIXED PEPPER BARQUETTES

Crisp pre-baked cases are given a moist and juicy filling of strips of red and yellow pepper. Basil leaves make an attractive garnish as well as adding to the scent and flavour of the barquettes.

See page 105 for recipe.

MEDITERRANEAN TARTLETS

Pre-baked tartlets full of Mediterranean flavours: a thick tomato mixture with black olives, and diced feta cheese with rocket and sundried tomatoes. They make an excellent first course or party snack.

See page 105 for recipes.

BLUE CHEESE & ONION FLAN WITH ALMONDS

Blue cheese gives this flan a distinctive tangy flavour, with which sweet tasting crunchy almonds contrast well. You could, however, use another cheese instead, such as mature Cheddar for a smoother flavour.

See page 105 for recipe.

STIR-FRIES

The classic Eastern way of cooking fresh vegetables is to chop them finely and fry them quickly and vigorously in hot, fragrant oil. It is a healthy method, cooking the vegetables so fast that they retain their individual tastes and firm texture. For a successful stir-fry, it is important to prepare all the ingredients before you start to cook, get the oil smoking hot before you add them, and cook them briefly, stirring continuously. Served with rice, a stir-fry makes a complete main course. This stir-fry is Thai-style with lemongrass, star anise, chilli, lime, fresh coriander and soy sauce. You can use all or some of these flavourings, according to taste and availability. This recipe serves 4.

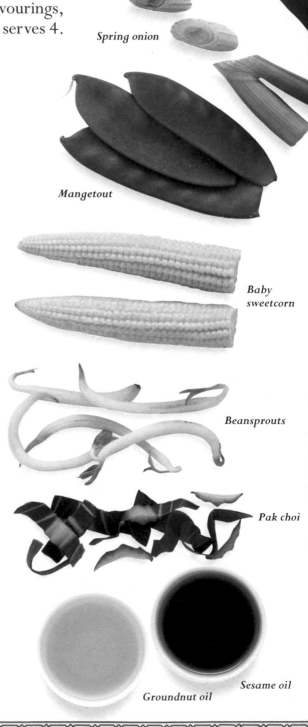

Spring onion

Mangetout

Baby sweetcorn

Beansprouts

Pak choi

Sesame oil

Groundnut oil

THAI-STYLE STIR-FRY VEGETABLES

INGREDIENTS

15ml (1 tbsp) sesame oil
15ml (1 tbsp) groundnut oil
175g (6oz) pak choi, shredded
250g (8oz) beansprouts
125g (4oz) baby sweetcorn
125g (4oz) mangetout, trimmed
small bunch of spring onions, chopped
1 red pepper, cored, deseeded and thinly sliced
125g (4oz) button mushrooms, sliced, or straw
mushrooms (from a jar or can), kept whole
1 stalk of lemongrass, white part finely sliced
1 fresh green chilli, deseeded and finely chopped
1 or 2 whole pods of star anise, seeds removed
and crushed
15ml (1 tbsp) soy sauce
juice and finely grated rind of 1 lime
2 – 3 tbsps chopped fresh coriander

PREPARATION

1 Pour the oils into a wok or a large frying pan and place over a high heat.
2 When the oils are smoking hot, drop in all the vegetables, the white part of the lemongrass, the chilli and the star anise seeds. As the vegetables fry, stir them vigorously with a long-handled wooden spoon until they are evenly heated through but still crisp: about 2 minutes.
3 Put in the soy sauce, lime juice and rind and coriander all at once. Stir again over the heat while they sizzle: just a few seconds. Serve at once.

Lime juice

Soy sauce

Star anise

Lime rind

Chilli

Lemongrass

Coriander

Mushrooms

Red pepper

ROULADES

Slices of roulade with their vivid spirals make an impressive course for a special meal. Most roulades gain texture and flavour from a semi-hard cheese, such as Gruyère, and are lightened by eggs. Variations include spinach, or cashew nuts, and one of the stunning roulades overleaf is an egg-free and cheese-free version made with red beans. The roulade here serves 6, as a starter, with fresh tomato sauce (page 121).

GRUYERE & HERB ROULADE WITH ASPARAGUS

INGREDIENTS

butter and dry grated Parmesan to coat the tin
175g (6oz) curd cheese
150ml (5fl oz) single cream
4 free-range eggs, separated
200g (7oz) Gruyère cheese, grated
3 tbsps chopped fresh herbs: chervil, flat-leaf parsley
salt and freshly ground black pepper
400g (14oz) asparagus tips

PREPARATION

1 Preheat the oven to 200°C/400°F/gas 6. Line a 22 x 32cm (9 x 13in) Swiss-roll tin with nonstick paper, butter it and dust with dry Parmesan.
2 Put 60g (2oz) of the curd cheese into a large bowl, add the cream and mix until smooth. Beat in the egg yolks one by one. Finally, stir in the Gruyère cheese and the herbs and season to taste.
3 In a separate bowl, whisk the egg whites until they are stiff but not so dry that you can slice them. Fold gently into the cheese mixture using a metal spoon. Pour this into the prepared tin, smoothing it to the edges, and bake until risen and just firm in the centre: 12–15 minutes.
4 Take the roulade out of the oven and turn it out, face down, on to nonstick paper sprinkled with the Parmesan. Peel the paper from the top.
5 Prepare the filling. Wash the asparagus well, break off and discard the tough stalk ends, then boil or steam until tender: 4–7 minutes.
6 Soften the remaining curd cheese with about 30ml (2 tbsps) water. Spread it over the roulade. Arrange the asparagus on top in rows, lining them up with the short side of the roulade. Roll up the roulade as shown on page 95.
7 Serve at once, cut into slices, or reheat wrapped in foil in a moderate oven, 180°C/350°F/gas 4, for 15 minutes or so.

Gruyère

Egg yolks

Single cream

Curd cheese

Flat-leaf parsley

Egg whites

Salt

Black pepper

Asparagus tips

Chervil

A SELECTION OF ROULADES

GRUYERE WITH RED PEPPERS

Sweet-tasting grilled red pepper makes a good filling for a Gruyère roulade and provides a bright colour contrast. Quick herb sauce (page 123), made with chives, goes well. Garnish with oregano.

See page 94 for recipe.

SPINACH WITH CREAM CHEESE & PEPPERS

Here a roulade of spinach is spread with cream cheese and irregularly placed strips of grilled red pepper. The colour and flavour of yellow pepper sauce (page 120) makes it the perfect accompaniment, and basil is a fragrant garnish.

See page 96 for recipe.

GRUYERE & HERBS WITH ROCKET

Peppery rocket contrasts well with the creamy-tasting avocado spread in this roulade. Other green leaves, such as watercress and lamb's lettuce, are excellent alternatives. Serve cold, with fresh tomato sauce (page 121), and garnish with rocket.

See page 94 for recipe.

RED BEAN ROULADE

The texture of this unusual roulade is softer than most. Serve it in slices on individual plates, rather than transferred whole to a serving dish, and gently reshape the slices using a palette knife. It is delicious served with an avocado sauce (page 123) and garnished with coriander.

See page 116 for recipe.

CHEDDAR & HERB WITH MUSHROOMS

Red wine sauce (page 121) complements this roulade well, and also makes it ideal for serving on a festive occasion such as Christmas. Any sort of mushroom can be used in the filling. Garnish with thyme.

See page 94 for recipe.

CASHEW NUT WITH BROCCOLI

This is a very rich roulade for a special occasion. Serve it with hollandaise sauce (page 123) and garnish simply with flat-leaf parsley. Pecans or really fresh walnuts (be careful to choose ones with no hint of bitterness) can replace the cashew nuts. For a lighter dish, serve with fromage frais.

See page 96 for recipe.

CREPES

L ight and delicious, crêpes can be layered, rolled or folded and filled with a wide variety of ingredients. Here crêpe cones are stuffed with leek and tarragon cream. Serves 4.

CREAMY LEEK & TARRAGON CREPES

INGREDIENTS

1 quantity of crêpe batter (page 149)
olive oil for cooking the crêpes
500g (1lb) trimmed leeks, sliced
400g (14oz) crème fraîche
1 tbsp chopped fresh flat-leaf parsley
2 tbsps chopped fresh tarragon
salt and freshly ground black pepper

PREPARATION

1 Preheat the oven to 180°C/350°F/gas 4 so that you can keep the crêpes warm once they are done. Place the batter and a ladle next to the hob.

2 Heat a small frying pan (about 15cm/6in across the base) and brush with olive oil. Once the oil is hot enough to sizzle when a drop of water is flicked into it, take it off the heat and, using the ladle, pour in enough batter – about 30ml (2 tbsps) – to coat the base. Return the pan to the heat and let the crêpe cook until the top is set and lightly browned: about 1 minute. Turn it over using a palette knife or spatula and your fingers.

3 Cook the second side until lightly browned: just a few seconds. Lift the crêpe out of the pan on to a piece of foil. Reheat the pan – you won't need to regrease it every time – and make the rest of the crêpes in the same way, stacking them up on foil. Cover with more foil and keep warm in the oven.

You can prepare the crêpes ahead of time. Wrap in foil and keep in the refrigerator for up to 3 days, or in the freezer for up to 3 months.

4 Cover the leeks with boiling water and cook until they are just tender: 5–7 minutes. Drain.

5 Put the leeks into a saucepan with the crème fraîche. Bring to the boil, reduce the heat and let the crème fraîche bubble away until it has reduced to a thick sauce and the leeks are tender: about 10 minutes. Stir in the herbs and season to taste.

6 Remove the warmed crêpes from the oven. Fold each one in half, then into quarters, spoon the filling under the top fold and serve.

Batter

Olive oil

Leeks

Crème fraîche

Flat-leaf parsley

Tarragon

Salt

Black pepper

RECIPES

This wonderfully eclectic collection is drawn from many different food cultures, proving that vegetarian cookery is truly international. Never again will anyone be able to say that vegetarian food is dull, after sampling such delights as tempura, gazpacho, couscous, falafel and spiced okra. Classic French dishes are well represented too, with soufflés, roulades, crêpes and terrines. One of the pleasures of vegetarian cookery is that dishes are flexible, so that they can play any part in a meal, from supporting role to main lead. To make life easier the menu planning section offers ideas for all sorts of occasions, from quick and easy suppers to formal dinner parties.

SOUPS

Soups are less complicated to make than many people imagine; some of the best classic soups are simply vegetables cooked gently in a little butter or olive oil, then simmered in water or stock until tender, and sieved, mashed or liquidized. Cream and chopped fresh herbs add a special touch. It is easy to make flavoursome vegetable stock, which freezes well, but even if you have none, don't be put off making soups: they can taste very good when made with just water, allowing the clear natural flavours to come through.

VEGETABLE STOCK

Make a habit of saving the water in which vegetables are cooked, and you will have a constant supply of excellent stock. To make stock from scratch, however, use odds and ends of vegetables, as here. Makes about 1 litre (1¾ pints).

INGREDIENTS

*1kg (2lb) mixed vegetables, such as onions, celery,
carrot trimmings, leek trimmings, parsley stalks
several cloves garlic, unpeeled
2 bay leaves
1 tbsp black peppercorns
1 or 2 sprigs of thyme
strip of lemon peel, optional*

PREPARATION

1 Put all the ingredients into a large saucepan or pot, cover with about 1.25 litres (2¼ pints) water, bring to the boil, then cover and leave to simmer until the vegetables are soft: 30–40 minutes.
2 Leave to cool. Strain through a sieve and keep in a covered container in the refrigerator. Use a batch of stock within four days. Alternatively, freeze in small amounts and use as required.

VARIATION

For a dark, richly flavoured stock, add some mushroom trimmings or chopped whole mushrooms to the saucepan or pot.

FRESH TOMATO SOUP

This is the easiest and most delicious tomato soup I know. It is best made in the summer when fresh tomatoes are abundant and deliciously ripe. Use fresh tomatoes; canned tomatoes won't do. Fresh tomato soup is also excellent chilled, made with olive oil instead of butter. Serves 4.

INGREDIENTS

*30g (1oz) butter **or** 30ml (2 tbsps) olive oil
(see note above)
1 medium-sized onion, chopped
2kg (4lb) fresh tomatoes, quartered
salt and freshly ground black pepper
pinch of sugar
150ml (5fl oz) single cream, optional
a few basil leaves, optional*

PREPARATION

1 Melt the butter or warm the oil in a large pan over a moderate heat, add the onion, cover and cook until the onion begins to soften: 5 minutes.
2 Add the tomatoes to the pan, cover and continue to cook until the tomatoes have collapsed and are purée-like: 10–15 minutes.
3 Pour the soup into a food processor or blender and work to a purée, then pass it through a sieve into a clean pan (to serve warm) or into a bowl (to serve chilled), adding a little water to thin it to the desired consistency if necessary. Season with salt and black pepper to taste, and stir in the sugar.
4 Reheat gently, or serve chilled from the refrigerator. If you like, swirl some cream into each bowl and strew a few basil leaves on top.

MUSHROOM, CHEESE & PARSLEY SOUP

This is a quick soup to make. Although I think it is best liquidized, it is also good left just as it is, in which case the cheese should be served separately for everyone to help themselves. A good vegetable stock enhances this soup, but it can also be made with just water, especially if the cheese is strong. Serves 4.

INGREDIENTS

15g (½oz) butter
15ml (1 tbsp) olive oil
1 medium-sized onion, chopped
1 large or 2 medium-sized cloves garlic, chopped
500g (1lb) mushrooms, sliced
600ml (1 pint) vegetable stock or water
150ml (5fl oz) single cream
4 tbsps finely chopped fresh flat-leaf parsley
salt and freshly ground black pepper
90g (3oz) finely grated Cheddar cheese

PREPARATION

1 Melt the butter with the oil in a large saucepan over a moderate heat, add the onion, cover and cook until the onion begins to soften: 5 minutes.
2 Add the garlic and mushrooms to the pan and cook, uncovered, until the mushrooms are tender: 5–10 minutes.
3 Pour in the stock or water, bring to the boil, cover and cook gently until the vegetables are very tender: about 10 minutes. Remove from the heat and stir in the cream and parsley.
4 If you prefer not to liquidize the soup, season it now with salt and black pepper and serve it straightaway, handing out the cheese separately.
5 To liquidize the soup, add the cheese, pour the soup into a food processor or blender and work until the mushrooms are finely chopped. Taste and season with salt and black pepper. Return to the pan, reheat gently (don't let it boil) and serve.

SPINACH SOUP WITH TOASTED PINENUTS

Tender spinach leaves make a delicious green soup, just right for spring and summer. A topping of toasted pinenuts adds an interesting texture and flavour; you can also use toasted flaked almonds if desired. For a slightly sharper flavour, replace a few of the spinach leaves with the same quantity of sorrel. Serves 4.

INGREDIENTS

15g (½oz) butter
15ml (1 tbsp) olive oil
1 medium-sized onion, chopped
400g (14oz) tender spinach leaves
600ml (1 pint) vegetable stock or water
150ml (5fl oz) single cream
freshly grated nutmeg
salt and freshly ground black pepper
60g (2oz) pinenuts

PREPARATION

1 Melt the butter with the oil in a large saucepan over a moderate heat, add the onion, cover and cook until the onion begins to soften: 5 minutes. Add the spinach, cover and cook until it has wilted: another 5 minutes.
2 Pour in the stock or water, bring to the boil, cover and cook gently until the spinach and onion are very tender: about 15 minutes. Remove from the heat and stir in the cream.
3 Pour the soup into a food processor or blender and liquidize it. Add a little water to thin it to the desired consistency, then season well with nutmeg, salt and black pepper. Return the soup to the pan and reheat gently (don't let it boil).
4 While the soup is reheating, toast the pinenuts under the grill until golden brown: 1–2 minutes. Keep an eye on them; they toast quickly.
5 Ladle the soup into bowls and sprinkle toasted pinenuts over each serving.

CLASSIC MINESTRONE

Served with grated cheese on top and plenty of good bread, this soup makes a complete main course. It is also delicious reheated and eaten the following day. Serves 4.

INGREDIENTS

60ml (4 tbsps) olive oil
1 large onion, chopped
3 sticks celery, finely diced
3 large carrots, finely diced
400g (14oz) can whole peeled tomatoes in juice
3 cloves garlic, chopped
3 tbsps tomato purée
3 large potatoes, peeled and diced
90g (3oz) medium-sized pasta, such as
maccheroni, boccolotti or farfalle
salt and freshly ground black pepper
small bunch of fresh flat-leaf parsley, chopped

PREPARATION

1 Warm the oil in a large saucepan over a moderate heat, add the onion, celery and carrots, cover and cook for 10 minutes.
2 Pour in the tomatoes, breaking them up with a wooden spoon, then add the garlic, tomato purée and just under 2 litres (3 pints) of water. Bring to the boil, cover and cook gently for 10 minutes.
3 Add the potatoes, bring back to the boil, then cook gently for a further 10 minutes.
4 Drop in the pasta and cook until the pasta and potatoes are tender: about 10 more minutes. Season with salt and black pepper to taste, and stir in the parsley just before serving.

VARIATIONS

Cabbage is good added to the soup, as are leeks, celeriac, courgettes and green beans. Canned white beans, such as cannellini or haricot, and chickpeas make filling additions: use the liquid in the can to dilute the soup if necessary.

BEETROOT & APPLE SOUP WITH HORSERADISH CREAM

Using cooked, skinned beetroot saves time but make sure that you buy the kind that has been prepared without vinegar. This soup, a variation on the classic soup borsch, is lovely for late summer or early autumn; serve it hot or chilled, depending on the weather. Serves 4.

INGREDIENTS

15g (½oz) butter
15ml (1 tbsp) olive oil
1 medium-sized onion, chopped
2 dessert apples, peeled, cored and sliced
150g (5oz) potato, peeled and diced
350g (12oz) cooked beetroot, diced
tiny pinch of ground cloves
salt and freshly ground black pepper
squeeze of lemon juice
150ml (5fl oz) soured cream
1 – 2 tsps creamed horseradish

PREPARATION

1 Melt the butter with the oil in a large saucepan over a moderate heat, add the onion, cover and cook until tender: 5 minutes. Add the apple and potato, stir well and reduce the heat. Cover and cook for a further 10 – 15 minutes.
2 Add the beetroot together with just under 1 litre (1½ pints) of water. Bring to the boil, cover and cook gently until the vegetables are very tender: about 15 minutes.
3 Pour the soup into a food processor or blender and liquidize. Add a little more water to thin the soup to the desired consistency, season with ground cloves, salt and black pepper, and use a squeeze or two of lemon juice to lift the flavour.
4 To serve warm, return to the pan and reheat gently (don't let it boil). To serve cold, transfer to a bowl, allow to cool and chill in the refrigerator.
5 Pour the cream into a small bowl and stir in enough creamed horseradish to give it a good tang. Serve the soup in individual bowls with the horseradish cream swirled on top.

VARIATIONS

CHILLED BEETROOT SOUP WITH ORANGE
Make the soup as described and chill. Stir in the grated rind and juice of half an orange, check the seasoning and serve, without horseradish cream.
BEETROOT & CABBAGE SOUP This is more like a traditional borsch. Replace the apple with 250g (8oz) shredded cabbage, and don't purée the soup but serve it chunky. Soured cream is the traditional accompaniment.

GAZPACHO

This Spanish summer soup needs no cooking. Serves 4.

INGREDIENTS

1 red onion
1 green pepper, cored and deseeded
½ large cucumber
500g (1lb) tomatoes, peeled and quartered
60g (2oz) stale white bread
2 cloves garlic
30ml (2 tbsps) red wine vinegar
30ml (2 tbsps) olive oil
salt and freshly ground black pepper
1 large ripe plum tomato
croûtons (page 47), optional

PREPARATION

1 Cut the onion, pepper and cucumber into large chunks. Put into a food processor or blender and chop briefly, keeping the texture chunky.

2 Transfer a quarter of the chopped vegetables to a bowl to serve separately later. Cover the bowl and keep it in the refrigerator.

3 Add the tomatoes, bread, garlic, vinegar and olive oil to the remainder of the vegetables in the food processor. Blend once more, briefly.

4 If necessary, add enough cold water to the soup mixture to lighten it without making it too thin. Season with salt and black pepper. Transfer to a large serving bowl, cover and place in the refrigerator to chill.

You can prepare ahead up to this point. The soup keeps for up to 24 hours in the refrigerator.

5 Finely chop the plum tomato and add it to the bowl of reserved vegetables.

6 Check and adjust the seasoning of the soup as chilling dulls its flavour. Ladle the soup into a chilled bowl and serve at once. Serve the bowl of reserved vegetables separately and also, if liked, a bowl of croûtons.

CUCUMBER & TARRAGON SOUP

Delicate in flavour, warm or chilled, this soup serves 4.

INGREDIENTS

1 cucumber, peeled and cut into chunks
1 medium-sized onion, chopped
1 clove garlic, peeled
8 – 10 sprigs of fresh tarragon, half of them chopped
1 litre (1¾ pints) vegetable stock or water
1 tbsp cornflour
150ml (5fl oz) single cream
30ml (2 tbsps) lemon juice
freshly grated nutmeg, salt, freshly ground black pepper

PREPARATION

1 Put the cucumber, onion, garlic, unchopped tarragon and stock or water into a saucepan. Bring to the boil and simmer until the cucumber is tender: about 15 minutes. Allow to cool slightly.
2 Liquidize in a food processor or blender. Return to the pan and bring back to the boil.
3 In a small bowl, mix the cornflour to a smooth paste with a little of the cream, then stir in the rest of the cream. Pour into the soup and stir over a moderate heat until the soup has thickened slightly: 2 – 3 minutes.
4 Add the chopped tarragon, lemon juice, nutmeg, salt and black pepper. Serve at once, warm, or transfer to a bowl to serve later, chilled.

POTATO & LEEK SOUP

Sieving this soup after liquidizing it gives it an extra-smooth texture. Try it warm or chilled; chilled it usually goes by the name vichyssoise. Serves 4.

INGREDIENTS

15ml (1 tbsp) olive oil
1 medium-sized onion, chopped
500g (1lb) potatoes, peeled and diced
500g (1lb) trimmed leeks, sliced
1 litre (1¾ pints) vegetable stock or water
150ml (5fl oz) single cream
freshly grated nutmeg, salt, freshly ground black pepper
chopped fresh chives, to taste

PREPARATION

1 Warm the oil in a large saucepan over a moderate heat, add the onion, cover and cook for 5 minutes. Add the potatoes and leeks, stir well, cover again and cook for a further 5 – 10 minutes.
2 Pour in the stock or water, bring to the boil and simmer until the vegetables are tender: about 15 minutes. Allow to cool slightly.
3 Liquidize in a food processor or blender, then pass through a sieve back into the pan (to serve warm) or into a bowl (to serve chilled).
4 Stir in the cream and season with nutmeg, salt and black pepper. Reheat gently, or serve chilled from the refrigerator, with chives on top.

WATERCRESS SOUP

This is delicious warm or chilled. Serves 4.

INGREDIENTS

15ml (1 tbsp) olive oil
1 medium-sized onion, chopped
500g (1lb) potatoes, peeled and diced
1 litre (1¾ pints) vegetable stock or water
75g (2½oz) watercress, trimmed and roughly chopped
150ml (5fl oz) single cream
freshly grated nutmeg, salt, freshly ground black pepper

PREPARATION

1 Warm the oil in a large saucepan over a moderate heat, add the onion, cover and cook for 5 minutes. Add the potatoes, stir well, cover again and cook for a further 5 – 10 minutes.
2 Pour in the stock or water, bring to the boil, then cover and cook gently until the potato is tender: about 15 minutes. Remove from the heat and stir in the watercress.
3 Liquidize in a food processor or blender. Return to the pan (to serve warm) or transfer to a bowl and refrigerate (to serve chilled).
4 Stir in the cream and season with nutmeg, salt and black pepper. Reheat gently, or serve chilled from the refrigerator.

VARIATION

JERUSALEM ARTICHOKE SOUP Replace the potato with the same weight of artichoke, which should be diced and then tossed in lemon juice to prevent it discolouring, and omit the watercress. Apart from these changes, make and serve in exactly the same way as the Watercress soup.

ACCOMPANIMENTS FOR SOUPS

CROUTONS

Sprinkled on soups and salads, croûtons add extra flavour and texture. Use slices of stale bread, with the crusts discarded and the bread cut into cubes. Fry the cubes in generous amounts of melted butter and olive oil until golden and crisp all over. Serve them at once, or make them ahead of time and warm them through in the oven before serving.

MELBA TOAST

These crisp triangles of thin toast are most easily made from ready-sliced bread. Toast several slices as you would to make ordinary toast. Cut through each slice horizontally to make two thin slices, toasted on one side. Cut into four triangles. Return to the hot grill, uncooked side up, and toast until speckled dark and slightly curled up.

BRUSCHETTA

This is the Italian country version of garlic bread, and it is perfect with minestrone. You need slices of coarse-textured Italian bread, such as ciabatta, a fat clove of garlic cut in half, and olive oil. Simply slice the bread, toast on both sides, rub with the cut clove of garlic, brush with olive oil and serve.

GARLIC OR HERB BREAD

For a typically sized French stick, you need about 90g (3oz) butter. For garlic bread, use 2 to 4 fat cloves of garlic, according to taste. Chop the garlic finely and mash it into the butter.

For herb bread, finely chop fresh herbs such as parsley, chives, oregano and marjoram, and mash about 2 tablespoons of them into the butter.

Preheat the oven to 200°C/400°F/gas 6. Cut into the French stick at 2.5cm (1in) intervals without going right through to the base, and press the garlic or herb butter into each crevice.

Wrap in foil, in two parcels if the bread fits the oven better that way, and bake until fragrant and hot inside and crisp outside: about 20 minutes.

CROSTINI

Small crunchy rounds of French bread with savoury spreads make a piquant accompaniment to soups. Crostini are particularly good with Olive and almond spread or Sundried tomato spread (right), or topped with morsels such as cheese, or mushrooms cooked in butter and garlic.

Preheat the oven to 160°C/325°F/gas 3. Take a slim French stick and cut it into slices about 1cm (½in) thick. Place them on a baking sheet and dry out in the oven: 10–15 minutes. Brush the slices on both sides with olive oil and return to the oven to crisp. Allow to cool before adding any topping.

OLIVE & ALMOND SPREAD

Rich and concentrated, a little of this spread goes a long way. Mix all the ingredients together into a smooth paste, softening with a little water if necessary, and serve, spread on crostini, as a snack to go with soup.

INGREDIENTS

100g (3½oz) black olive purée or well-mashed olives
100g (3½oz) ground almonds
4 tbsps finely chopped capers
salt and freshly ground black pepper

VARIATION

SUNDRIED TOMATO SPREAD Replace the black olives with the same weight of sundried tomatoes in oil, puréed or well mashed. Omit the capers, and add some roughly chopped basil.

SALADS

A salad can be a refreshing accompaniment to a main dish, or the distinctive centrepiece of a meal; composed of cooked or raw ingredients; even served warm as well as at room temperature. It is probably the most versatile dish in the kitchen, providing endless possibilities for different combinations of colour, flavour and texture. With such a diversity of salad leaves, oils and vinegars available, you can enjoy trying out new recipes or experimenting with your own ideas. Leaves are often a key ingredient: store them in the refrigerator where they will keep for several days, then wash and spin, shake or blot dry on kitchen paper just before use.

CHICORY, WATERCRESS, FENNEL, RED ONION & ORANGE SALAD

This combination of ingredients is particularly refreshing in both colour and flavour. The salad does not contain vinegar because the juice of the oranges mingles with the oil to make a light dressing. Serves 4.

INGREDIENTS

1 clove garlic, peeled and halved
45ml (3 tbsps) olive oil
salt and freshly ground black pepper
`2 – 3 oranges, peel and pith removed, cut on
a plate into rounds
2 heads of chicory, broken apart
75 – 100g (about 3oz) watercress, tough stems removed
1 fennel bulb, thinly sliced
1 red onion, sliced into thin rings

PREPARATION

1 Rub the garlic halves around the salad bowl and then discard them. Or, for a stronger garlic flavour, crush the garlic and place it in the bowl.
2 Put the oil and a good seasoning of salt and pepper into the bowl. Mix lightly with a fork.
3 Add the orange slices, along with the juice that has collected in the plate.
4 Put the chicory and watercress (torn a little if you wish) into the bowl on top of the oranges and dressing. Finally add the fennel and the onion.
5 Toss the salad gently. Serve at once.

Orange

Black pepper

Salt

Olive oil

Garlic

Watercress

Fennel

Red onion

Chicory

FEUILLE DE CHENE, AVOCADO & ROASTED CASHEW NUTS

It is important to assemble this salad just before you serve it so the leaves and cashew nuts remain crisp and the avocado keeps its colour. Serves 4 as a first course or accompaniment, 2 as a main course.

INGREDIENTS

1 feuille de chêne lettuce
1 clove garlic, peeled and halved
15ml (1 tbsp) red wine vinegar
45ml (3 tbsps) olive oil
salt and freshly ground black pepper
1 ripe avocado
30ml (2 tbsps) lemon juice
2 tbsps chopped fresh chives
125g (4oz) roasted cashew nuts

PREPARATION

1 Wash and spin or blot dry the feuille de chêne salad leaves.
2 Rub the garlic halves around the salad bowl and then discard them. Or, for a stronger garlic flavour, crush the garlic and place it in the bowl.
3 Put the vinegar, oil and a good seasoning of salt and pepper into the bowl. Mix lightly with a fork.
4 Halve the avocado, remove the peel and the stone and slice the flesh. Place in a bowl, sprinkle with the lemon juice and season with a little salt and black pepper.
5 Tear the salad leaves and scatter them on top of the dressing in the bowl. Add the chives, avocado and cashew nuts. Toss the salad so that the leaves are lightly coated with dressing and serve at once.

NEW POTATO SALAD

Although new potatoes are best for this, you can use any waxy potatoes that won't break up. Serves 4.

INGREDIENTS

750g (1½lb) new potatoes or waxy potatoes, scrubbed
15ml (1 tbsp) wine vinegar
45ml (3 tbsps) olive oil
salt and freshly ground black pepper
2 tbsps mayonnaise (for homemade see page 122)
30ml (2 tbsps) Greek yogurt or soured cream
2 tbsps chopped fresh chives

PREPARATION

1 Boil the potatoes until they are just tender, then drain. Either leave the skins on – delicious on new potatoes – or pull them off the potatoes when cool. Cut large potatoes into pieces.
2 Put the vinegar, oil and a good seasoning of salt and pepper into a bowl. Mix lightly with a fork. Add the potatoes and turn them over gently in the dressing. Leave to cool completely.

🕐 *You can prepare ahead up to this point. The salad keeps up to 24 hours in a covered container in the refrigerator.*

3 Add the mayonnaise, yogurt or cream and half of the chives to the bowl and mix gently. Taste and adjust the seasoning if necessary.
4 Transfer to a serving bowl, scatter the remaining chives on top, and serve.

WHITE CABBAGE SALAD

Cabbage salad, or coleslaw, can be served immediately or kept in a covered container in the refrigerator for 24 hours. The flavour improves with keeping. Serves 4.

INGREDIENTS

350g (12oz) white cabbage, shredded
125g (4oz) carrots, grated
1 shallot or small mild onion, finely chopped
2 tbsps mayonnaise (for homemade see page 122)
30ml (2 tbsps) Greek yogurt or soured cream
2 tbsps chopped fresh chives or other fresh herbs
salt and freshly ground black pepper

PREPARATION

1 Mix the vegetables together in a large bowl.
2 Add the mayonnaise, yogurt or cream, herbs and a good seasoning of salt and black pepper. Combine well. Serve at once or keep for later.

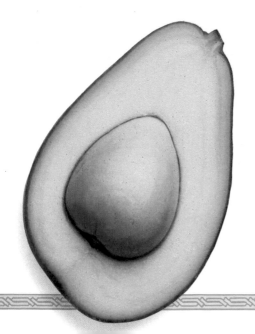

INSALATA TRICOLORE

Taking its name from the Italian flag, this three-coloured salad is particularly good as an accompaniment for pasta. Serves 4.

INGREDIENTS

500g (1lb) fresh ripe plum tomatoes
2 ripe avocados
250g (8oz) mozzarella cheese, sliced
salt and freshly ground black pepper
several sprigs of fresh basil
15ml (1 tbsp) red wine vinegar
45ml (3 tbsps) olive oil

PREPARATION

1 Cut the tomatoes either across into rounds or downwards into long thin slices, cutting out any hard pieces of core.
2 Halve the avocados, remove the peel and the stone and slice the flesh.
3 On individual plates, arrange alternating slices of tomato, avocado and mozzarella cheese. Season with salt and black pepper, then tear the basil leaves and sprinkle them over the top.
4 Mix together the vinegar and the oil and spoon over the salads. Serve at once.

RED & YELLOW CHERRY TOMATOES WITH ORANGE & THYME

This pretty salad makes a change from the more usual tomato and basil salads. It is best made at least half an hour before you want to eat it. Keep it in a cool place but not in the refrigerator, where its flavour would become dulled. Serves 4.

INGREDIENTS

250g (8oz) red cherry tomatoes, halved
250g (8oz) yellow cherry tomatoes, halved
60g (2oz) small black olives, such as niçoise olives
1 tbsp chopped fresh thyme
15ml (1 tbsp) olive oil
juice and finely grated rind of 1 small orange
salt and freshly ground black pepper

PREPARATION

1 Put all the ingredients into a bowl and mix them lightly together.
2 Leave to stand for at least 30 minutes in a cool place (not the refrigerator), then mix again. Check the seasoning and serve.

PLUM TOMATOES WITH BASIL

Make this a little ahead of time if you can so that the juices run and the flavours mingle. Keep it in a cool place but not in the refrigerator; serve at room temperature for the flavours to be at their best. Serves 4.

INGREDIENTS

500g (1lb) fresh ripe plum tomatoes
15ml (1 tbsp) red wine vinegar
45ml (3 tbsps) olive oil
salt and freshly ground black pepper
several sprigs of fresh basil

PREPARATION

1 Cut the tomatoes either across into rounds or downwards into long thin slices, cutting out any hard pieces of core. Place in a shallow dish.
2 Sprinkle with vinegar, oil, salt and black pepper. Tear the basil leaves and scatter them over the top. Mix the ingredients lightly together.
3 Serve at once or keep in a cool place for later. If serving later, mix again and check the seasoning.

GRILLED PEPPERS WITH BASIL

This richly flavoured salad benefits from being made several hours in advance. Serves 4.

INGREDIENTS

4 large red and yellow peppers, quartered
2 tsps balsamic vinegar
15ml (1 tbsp) olive oil
salt and freshly ground black pepper
several sprigs of fresh basil

PREPARATION

1 Grill and peel the peppers as shown on page 144. Remove the stalk and seeds, and cut the flesh into strips. Place the strips in a shallow dish.
2 Sprinkle with vinegar, oil, salt and black pepper. Tear the basil leaves and scatter them over the top. Mix the ingredients lightly together.
3 Serve at once or keep in a cool place for later. If served later, mix again and check the seasoning.

MIXED LEAF SALAD WITH FLOWERS & HERBS

Without doubt, this is my most useful salad; indeed, it is probably my most versatile vegetable accompaniment. It is quick, health-giving and seems to go with every sort of main course. For variety, add mustard or garlic, flakes of Parmesan, cubes of Gruyère, toasted nuts or croûtons. Illustrated on pages 54–5. Serves 4.

INGREDIENTS

250g (8oz) mixed salad leaves, such as feuille de chêne, lollo rosso, frisée, lamb's lettuce, radicchio
30g (1oz) rocket or other strongly flavoured leaves such as baby nasturtium leaves, dandelion leaves
2 tsps balsamic vinegar
1 tsp red wine vinegar
45ml (3 tbsps) olive oil
salt and freshly ground black pepper
1 tbsp chopped fresh tarragon
1 tbsp chopped fresh chives
1 tbsp chopped fresh flat-leaf parsley
125g (4oz) nasturtium flowers or mixed flowers

PREPARATION

1 Wash and spin or blot dry all the leaves.
2 Put the vinegars, oil and a good seasoning of salt and black pepper into a large bowl – you can use the one that you are planning to serve the salad from – and mix lightly with a fork.
3 Cross the salad servers in the base of the bowl, then put in the salad leaves, the herbs and the flowers. Leave the salad like this, with the crossed salad servers lifting the delicate leaves, herbs and flowers out of the dressing, until just before you want to eat the salad.
4 Toss the salad with the servers, so that all the leaves are lightly coated with dressing, then serve and eat at once.

GREEN LEAVES WITH GOAT'S CHEESE & WALNUTS

This leafy green salad has grilled goat's cheese added to it at the last minute. Make sure the walnuts are fresh and have no trace of bitterness. Serves 4.

INGREDIENTS

2 lettuces of different types, such as feuille de chêne and frisée, or 250g (8oz) mixed salad leaves
1 clove garlic, peeled and halved
15ml (1 tbsp) red wine vinegar
30ml (2 tbsps) olive oil
15ml (1 tbsp) walnut oil
salt and freshly ground black pepper
125g (4oz) fresh walnut halves or pieces
250g (8oz) firm goat's cheese (the type usually sold in a log), thinly sliced

PREPARATION

1 Wash and spin or blot dry the salad leaves.
2 Rub the garlic halves around the salad bowl and then discard them. Or, for a stronger garlic flavour, crush the garlic and place it in the bowl.
3 Put the vinegar, oils and a good seasoning of salt and pepper into the bowl. Mix lightly with a fork.
4 Toast the walnuts on a baking sheet under a hot grill until they are lightly browned: 2–3 minutes. Set them aside; leave the grill on the same setting.
5 Toast the goat's cheese on one side on a baking sheet until it is flecked with brown and beginning to melt: 1–2 minutes.
6 Tear the salad leaves and place in the bowl on top of the dressing, add the walnuts and toss lightly. Distribute among individual plates and put the melting cheese on top. Serve and eat at once.

ROCKET SALAD WITH FLAKES OF PARMESAN

This delicious, full-bodied mixture of flavours goes particularly well with pasta dishes. Serves 4.

INGREDIENTS

250g (8oz) rocket
1 clove garlic, peeled and halved
15ml (1 tbsp) red wine vinegar
45ml (3 tbsps) olive oil
salt and freshly ground black pepper
125g (4oz) Parmesan cheese, cut into flakes

PREPARATION

1 Wash and spin or blot dry the rocket.
2 Rub the garlic halves around the salad bowl and then discard them. Or, for a stronger garlic flavour, crush the garlic and place it in the bowl.
3 Put the vinegar, oil and a good seasoning of salt and pepper into the bowl. Mix lightly with a fork.
4 Add the rocket, toss it gently in the dressing, scatter the Parmesan over the top and serve.

VEGETARIAN SALADE NIÇOISE

With crusty bread, this makes a filling meal for 4. Illustrated on page 54.

INGREDIENTS

250g (8oz) green beans, trimmed
500g (1lb) fresh ripe plum tomatoes
15ml (1 tbsp) wine vinegar
60ml (4 tbsps) olive oil
salt and freshly ground black pepper
400g (14oz) can artichoke hearts,
drained and quartered
4 free-range eggs, hardboiled and cut into wedges
4 tbsps chopped fresh flat-leaf parsley
125g (4oz) black olives

PREPARATION

1 Place the green beans in a small pan, cover with boiling water and cook until just tender: 2−4 minutes. Drain and refresh under cold water.
2 Cut the tomatoes either across into rounds or downwards into long thin slices, cutting out any hard pieces of core.
3 Put the vinegar, oil and a good seasoning of salt and pepper into a bowl. Mix lightly with a fork.
4 Add the beans, tomatoes and remaining ingredients to the bowl, stir gently and serve.

BEAN & HERB SALAD

Served with bread, this makes a satisfying, light main course, and it can also be served as part of a buffet. A leafy green salad is a good accompaniment. Serves 4.

INGREDIENTS

350g (12oz) fresh podded or frozen broad beans
250g (8oz) green beans, trimmed
1 clove garlic, crushed
30ml (2 tbsps) wine vinegar
90ml (6 tbsps) olive oil
salt and freshly ground black pepper
400g (14oz) can cannellini or haricot beans, drained
400g (14oz) can chickpeas, drained
3 tbsps chopped fresh herbs, such as
flat-leaf parsley, chives, mint

PREPARATION

1 Place the broad beans in a small pan, cover with boiling water and cook until just tender: 4−5 minutes. Drain. When cool enough to handle, pop them out of their skins with finger and thumb.
2 Place the green beans in a small pan, cover with boiling water and cook until just tender: 2−4 minutes. Drain and refresh under cold water.
3 Put the garlic in a bowl with the vinegar, oil and a good seasoning of salt and black pepper. Mix lightly with a fork to make the dressing.
4 Add the three kinds of beans, the chickpeas and the herbs. Toss gently to coat them well.

 You can prepare ahead to this point. The salad keeps for up to 48 hours in a covered container in the refrigerator.

5 Allow the salad to rest at room temperature for at least an hour, stirring from time to time, so that the flavours develop, then serve.

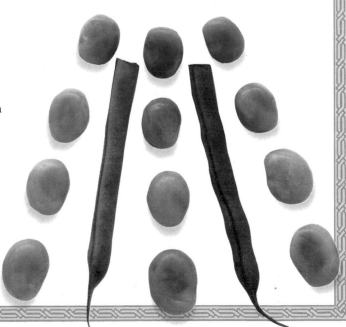

Vegetarian salade niçoise (page 53)

Tabbouleh (page 57)

*Mixed leaf salad
with flowers and
herbs (page 52)*

WARM PASTA SALAD WITH TOMATO & BASIL

*A quick and filling main course dish for 4.
It gains richness of flavour from avocado or mozzarella
cheese; you could even use both.*

INGREDIENTS

*500g (1lb) fresh ripe plum tomatoes
500g (1lb) fusilli or other small chunky pasta
45ml (3 tbsps) olive oil
salt and freshly ground black pepper
250g (8oz) mozzarella cheese, sliced, **or** flesh of 2 ripe
avocados, sprinkled with lemon juice
several sprigs of fresh basil
Parmesan cheese, cut into flakes, optional*

PREPARATION

1 Pour 4 litres (7 pints) of water into a large pan
and place over a high heat for the pasta.
2 Cut the tomatoes either across into rounds or
downwards into long thin slices, cutting out any
hard pieces of core.
3 When the water reaches a rolling boil, drop in
the pasta. Bring back to the boil, give the pasta a
quick stir, then let the water boil steadily until the
pasta is *al dente*: tender but not soft right through.
Bite a piece to check.
4 Drain the pasta but leave some water clinging to
it, and put it back into the hot pan with the olive
oil and a good seasoning of salt and black pepper,
tossing the pasta so that it is coated with the oil.
5 Add the tomato and the mozzarella or avocado,
or both, to the pasta. Tear the basil and stir it in.
Check the seasoning and serve at once, strewn
with flakes of Parmesan if desired.

WARM PASTA SALAD WITH GRILLED PEPPER & ROCKET

*This simple, filling dish is colourful, full of the
Mediterranean flavours of rich, sweet peppers
and peppery rocket. Serves 4.*

INGREDIENTS

*4 large red and yellow peppers, quartered
500g (1lb) penne or other small chunky pasta
30ml (2 tbsps) olive oil
salt and freshly ground black pepper
30g (1oz) rocket
Parmesan cheese, cut into flakes, optional*

PREPARATION

1 Pour 4 litres (7 pints) of water into a large pan
and place over a high heat for the pasta.
2 Grill and peel the peppers as shown on page 144.
Remove the stalk and the seeds, and cut the flesh
into long strips.
3 When the water reaches a rolling boil, drop in
the pasta. Bring back to the boil, give the pasta a
quick stir, then let the water boil steadily until the
pasta is *al dente*: tender but not soft right through.
Bite a piece to check.
4 Drain the pasta but leave some water clinging to
it, and put it back into the hot pan with the olive
oil, multi-coloured pepper strips and a good
seasoning of salt and black pepper, tossing the
pasta so that it is coated with the oil and the
pepper strips are warmed through.
5 Tear the rocket roughly and add it to the pasta.
Toss gently to distribute the rocket well. Check
the seasoning and serve at once, strewn with flakes
of Parmesan if desired.

TABBOULEH

Allow this refreshing dish to stand so that the grains — I prefer couscous to bulgur — soften and absorb the flavours. Illustrated on page 55. Serves 4.

INGREDIENTS

250g (8oz) dry, unsoaked couscous or bulgur wheat
4 large tomatoes, roughly chopped
1 green pepper, cored, deseeded and roughly chopped
½ cucumber, roughly chopped
1 clove garlic, crushed
1 red onion, finely chopped
juice of 2 lemons
60ml (4 tbsps) olive oil
6 tbsps chopped fresh flat-leaf parsley
2–3 tbsps chopped fresh mint
salt and freshly ground black pepper

PREPARATION

1 Put the couscous or bulgur wheat into a bowl.
2 Add all the ingredients, season with salt and pepper, cover and refrigerate for 12–48 hours. Check and adjust seasoning before serving.

RICE SALAD WITH HERBS, AVOCADO & NUTS

An attractive, fragrant main dish for 4.

INGREDIENTS

250g (8oz) long grain brown or white rice
½ tsp turmeric powder
½ tsp sea salt, optional
juice and finely grated rind of ½ lemon
6 tbsps chopped mixed fresh herbs, such as
flat-leaf parsley, mint, chives and tarragon
1 large ripe avocado
60g (2oz) shelled pistachio nuts
60g (2oz) cashew nuts, toasted briefly under a hot grill
salt and freshly ground black pepper

PREPARATION

1 Cook the rice as described on page 152, adding turmeric, and sea salt if desired.
2 Add the lemon rind (reserve the juice for later) and herbs and stir the rice with a wooden fork, mixing them in gently. Leave until the rice is cold.
3 When you are almost ready to eat the salad, halve the avocado, remove the peel and stone and chop the flesh. Toss the avocado in the reserved lemon juice then add it to the salad, along with the nuts. Check the seasoning, and serve at once.

WHEAT GRAINS WITH APRICOTS & PINENUTS

This salad has a Middle Eastern flavour, but it is my own invention. It tastes best if kept in a cool place for several hours before being eaten. Serves 4.

INGREDIENTS

250g (8oz) wheat grains, brown rice or millet
30ml (2 tbsps) olive oil
2 red onions, sliced
250g (8oz) dried apricots, chopped
125g (4oz) raisins
30ml (2 tbsps) balsamic vinegar
2 tbsps chopped fresh flat-leaf parsley
2 tbsps chopped fresh mint
salt and freshly ground black pepper
125g (4oz) pinenuts, toasted briefly under a hot grill

PREPARATION

1 If using wheat grains, cover with cold water and leave to soak for 8 hours or overnight, then boil, covered, for 1¼ hours until tender, topping up the water as necessary. If using rice or millet, cook by the absorption method, as described on page 152, allowing only 15–20 minutes for the millet. Drain as necessary. Transfer to a serving bowl.
2 Warm the oil in a large saucepan over a moderate heat, add the onion, cover and cook gently until tender but still slightly crunchy: about 5 minutes. Remove from the heat and add the onion and its oil to the grains.
3 Add the apricots, raisins, balsamic vinegar, parsley and mint and mix well. Season to taste with salt and black pepper.
4 Stir in the toasted pinenuts, or scatter over the top of the salad, just before serving so that they retain their crispness. Serve at once.

VEGETABLE DIPS

Crudités, or pieces of raw vegetable, prepared simply, can be served with dips as part of a buffet, a snack with drinks, or an appetizer. Almost any vegetables may be used: sticks of cucumber, courgette, celery and carrot; strips of pepper; whole mangetout, baby sweetcorn, radishes, cherry tomatoes, button mushrooms, and so on. As well as the recipes here, try mayonnaise with herbs or garlic (page 122).

GOAT'S CHEESE DIP

Crudités are ideal for this dip; melba toast or garlicky bruschetta (page 47) are options too. Serves 2 to 4.

INGREDIENTS

125g (4oz) low-fat, smooth, soft white cheese
125g (4oz) firm goat's cheese with rind (the type usually sold in a log)
salt and freshly ground black pepper

PREPARATION

1 Put the soft white cheese into a bowl, add the goat's cheese with its rind and mash well until the consistency is smooth.
2 Season with salt and black pepper and spoon into a serving bowl.

VARIATION

BLUE CHEESE DIP Use 125g (4oz) of blue cheese instead of the goat's cheese: mash it into the soft white cheese as described above.

CUCUMBER & MINT DIP

This refreshing dip is perfect with crudités. Serves 2 to 4.

INGREDIENTS

½ cucumber, peeled and diced
salt
300ml (½ pint) Greek yogurt
1 – 2 tbsps chopped fresh mint
½ tsp wine vinegar
freshly ground black pepper

PREPARATION

1 Put the cucumber into a sieve, sprinkle with salt and leave for at least 30 minutes. This draws out some of the liquid so the dip is not watery.
2 Spoon the Greek yogurt into a bowl. Pat the cucumber dry on kitchen paper and mix with the yogurt. Add the mint, vinegar, and black pepper to taste. Stir gently and serve at once.

VARIATION

HERB DIP Replace the cucumber and mint with 4 tablespoons of chopped fresh herbs: tarragon, dill, fennel, basil, oregano, marjoram, coriander, chives, parsley and chervil are all possibilities. Instead of vinegar, use lemon juice.

GUACAMOLE

An authentic guacamole contains only avocado, fresh coriander, tomatoes and fresh chillies, seasoned with salt and black pepper — add anything else and it becomes an avocado dip. I sometimes serve it on a bed of salad leaves or with red bean dishes. Use really ripe avocados for the best result. Serves 4 to 6.

INGREDIENTS

2 – 3 fresh green chillies, deseeded and finely chopped
4 tomatoes, finely chopped
3 tbsps chopped fresh coriander
2 large ripe avocados
salt and freshly ground black pepper

PREPARATION

1 Place the chillies, tomatoes and coriander in a small bowl.

 You can prepare ahead up to this point. Cover and keep in a cool place until just before you are ready to serve.

2 At the last minute, halve the avocados and remove the stone. Scoop out the flesh and place it in the bowl with the chillies, tomatoes and coriander. Use a fork to mash the ingredients together well. Season to taste with salt and black pepper and serve at once.

CURRIED CASHEW NUT DIP

Crunchy and spicy, this dip goes well with sticks of celery and cucumber. Serves 2 to 4.

INGREDIENTS

15ml (1 tbsp) olive oil
1 small onion, chopped
1 clove garlic, chopped
2 tsps curry powder
150g (5oz) low-fat cream cheese
45g (1½oz) cashew nuts, toasted briefly under a hot grill
salt and freshly ground black pepper

PREPARATION

1 Warm the oil in a saucepan over a moderate heat, add the onion and garlic, cover and cook for 5 minutes. Stir in the curry powder and cook for a further 2 – 3 minutes. Remove from the heat.
2 Put the cheese, onion mixture and cashew nuts into a food processor or blender and chop finely. Transfer to a bowl for serving. Alternatively, put the cheese and onion in a bowl, finely chop the nuts and stir them in. Season and serve at once.

HUMMUS

Although hummus is quite widely available, it is so easy to make that if you have a food processor or blender you might as well try the tastier homemade version. Use a light tahini (sesame seed paste); the dark one is too bitter. Serves 2 to 4.

INGREDIENTS

400g (14oz) can chickpeas, drained, liquid reserved
1 – 2 cloves garlic
15ml (1 tbsp) light tahini (see note above)
30ml (2 tbsps) lemon juice
15ml (1 tbsp) olive oil
pinch of chilli powder, optional
salt and freshly ground black pepper
1 – 2 tbsps cumin seeds, optional

PREPARATION

1 Put the chickpeas, garlic, tahini, lemon juice and olive oil into a food processor or blender and purée until smooth. Pour in enough of the reserved chickpea liquid to make the consistency like that of lightly whipped cream – you will probably need most, if not all, of the liquid.
2 Add a pinch or two of chilli powder to give the hummus a bit of a kick, if desired, then season with salt and black pepper. Transfer to a bowl.
3 Fry the cumin seeds, if using, in a dry pan over a moderate heat until they smell aromatic and begin to pop: 1 – 2 minutes. Sprinkle over the hummus, and serve.

MUSHROOM DIP

Try this with melba toast (page 47). Serves 2 to 4.

INGREDIENTS

15g (½oz) butter
15ml (1 tbsp) olive oil
250g (8oz) button mushrooms, very finely chopped
1 small clove garlic, chopped
125g (4oz) curd cheese
1 tbsp chopped fresh flat-leaf parsley
salt and freshly ground black pepper

PREPARATION

1 Melt the butter with the oil in a large saucepan over a moderate heat and add the mushrooms and garlic. Cook until the mushrooms are tender and just browned: 5 minutes. Remove from the heat.
2 Beat the curd cheese in a bowl to soften it, then stir in the mushroom and garlic mixture and the parsley. Season and serve at once.

VEGETABLE DISHES

A hallmark of the new classic vegetarian cookery is exciting and colourful vegetable dishes, inspired by the cuisines of many cultures as well as by the fresh ingredients themselves. Some dishes, served with bread and a salad, are a satisfying meal on their own. Alternatively, put several together, giving as much variety as possible, for a feast.

VEGETABLES A LA GRECQUE

"Greek-style", or à la grecque, refers to vegetables cooked in olive oil with a little spice. The dish can be made ahead and served cold, so it is ideal for eating outdoors. Serves 4 as a first course, 2 as a main course.

INGREDIENTS

30ml (2 tbsps) olive oil
2 medium or 3 small fennel bulbs, feathery leaves reserved, thinly sliced
1 medium-sized onion, chopped
2 cloves garlic, chopped
1 tbsp coriander seeds
500g (1lb) tomatoes, peeled and chopped
½ medium-sized cauliflower, divided into florets
125g (4oz) green beans, trimmed
125g (4oz) button mushrooms, halved or quartered
salt and freshly ground black pepper
2 – 3 tbsps chopped fresh flat-leaf parsley

PREPARATION

1 Warm the oil in a large saucepan over a moderate heat, add the fennel (including its feathery leaves) and onion, cover and cook for 5 minutes. Add the garlic and cook for 1 minute.

2 Crush the coriander seeds and stir them into the fennel mixture, then add the tomatoes. Cook, uncovered, until the vegetables are tender and any liquid has evaporated: about 20 minutes.

3 Meanwhile, half-boil, half-steam the cauliflower and green beans: place in a pan, pour in boiling water to 1cm (½in) deep, cover and cook until just tender: 3 – 4 minutes. Drain immediately, refresh under cold running water and leave to dry.

4 Once the fennel and tomato mixture is ready, add the mushrooms and cook gently for a further 3 – 4 minutes. Stir in the cauliflower and green beans and season with salt and black pepper. Remove from the heat and set aside.

5 Serve at once, warm, or serve later at room temperature, sprinkled with parsley.

Coriander seeds

Garlic

Onion

Fennel

Olive oil

Cauliflower

Green beans

Mushrooms

Salt

Black pepper

Flat-leaf parsley

Tomatoes

MUSHROOM STROGANOFF

Use a variety of mushrooms: some wild ones, perhaps, or a mixture of oyster, chestnut and shiitake mushrooms, with button mushrooms to make up the weight. It will seem like a lot and you need a large saucepan, but they cook down considerably. Serve with boiled rice; for 4.

INGREDIENTS

30g (1oz) butter
15ml (1 tbsp) olive oil
2 large onions, chopped
2 cloves garlic, chopped
1kg (2lb) mushrooms (see introductory note), sliced
200g (7oz) crème fraîche
1 tsp tomato purée
freshly grated nutmeg
salt and freshly ground black pepper
paprika, to serve

PREPARATION

1 Melt the butter with the oil in a large saucepan over a moderate heat, add the onion, cover and cook for 5 minutes. Add the garlic and cook for another 2–3 minutes.
2 Add the mushrooms and cook, uncovered, over a moderate heat until the mushrooms are tender and much reduced and most of the liquid has evaporated: 20–30 minutes.
3 Stir the crème fraîche and tomato purée into the mixture, turn up the heat and bring to the boil. Allow to bubble for 1–2 minutes. Season with nutmeg, salt and black pepper and serve, sprinkled with paprika.

ROASTED PEPPER RATATOUILLE

Colourful and delicious, this is one of my standbys. You can eat it hot with new potatoes, rice, pasta or garlic bread, or cold as part of a salad meal. Serves 4.

INGREDIENTS

2 red and 2 yellow peppers, quartered
45ml (3 tbsps) olive oil
2 large onions, chopped
4 cloves garlic, chopped
2 green peppers, cored, deseeded and sliced into rounds
500g (1lb) courgettes, sliced
2 x 400g (14oz) cans whole peeled tomatoes, coarsely chopped, with juice
salt and freshly ground black pepper
chopped fresh flat-leaf parsley, to serve

PREPARATION

1 Grill and peel the red and yellow peppers as shown on page 144. Remove the stalk and seeds, and cut the flesh into strips. Set aside.
2 Warm the oil in a large pan over a moderate heat, add the onion, cover and cook for 5 minutes.
3 Add the garlic, green peppers and courgettes and stir well. Cook, stirring from time to time, for a further 5 minutes.
4 Pour in the tomatoes. Reduce the heat and let the mixture simmer, uncovered, until the vegetables are tender and much of the tomato liquid has evaporated: 20–30 minutes. Towards the end of the cooking time, stir in the red and yellow peppers and allow them to heat through.
5 Season and serve, sprinkled with parsley.

VEGETABLE BOURGUIGNON

Serve with baked potatoes for a warming meal for 4.

INGREDIENTS

30g (1oz) butter
15ml (1 tbsp) olive oil
*250g (8oz) button onions **or** 1 large onion, sliced*
4 cloves garlic, chopped
500g (1lb) carrots, sliced
4 large sticks of celery, sliced
500g (1lb) trimmed leeks, sliced
250g (8oz) baby button mushrooms
2 bay leaves
2 tbsps plain flour
600ml (1 pint) red wine
900ml (1½ pints) vegetable stock (page 42) or water
salt and freshly ground black pepper
chopped fresh flat-leaf parsley, to serve

PREPARATION

1 Melt the butter with the oil in a large, heavy-bottomed pan or casserole dish over a moderate heat, add the onion, cover and cook for 5 minutes.
2 Add the garlic, carrots, celery, leeks, mushrooms and bay leaves and stir well. Cover and cook for a further 5 minutes.
3 Sprinkle the flour over the vegetables. Stir over the heat with a wooden spoon for 1–2 minutes to cook the flour.
4 Pour in the wine and stock or water, raise the heat and bring to the boil. Reduce the heat, partially cover the pan and leave to simmer gently until the vegetables are tender and the liquid has reduced: about 1¼ hours.
5 Season to taste with salt and black pepper and serve, sprinkled with parsley.

CHILLI LIME AVOCADOS

It is important not to overcook these stuffed avocados. They should be left in the oven only long enough to heat through. Illustrated on page 24. Serves 4.

INGREDIENTS

*30ml (2 tbsps) olive oil
1 large onion, chopped
2 cloves garlic, chopped
1 – 2 fresh green chillies, deseeded and finely chopped
2 large ripe avocados
juice of 1 lime
2 tbsps chopped fresh chives
salt and freshly ground black pepper
thin slices of lime, to garnish*

PREPARATION

1 Preheat the oven to 200°C/400°F/gas 6.
2 Warm the oil in a saucepan over a moderate heat, add the onion and sauté until lightly browned: about 7 minutes.
3 Add the garlic and chillies, stir well and cook for 5 minutes. Remove from the heat.
4 Halve the avocados, remove the stones and scoop out the flesh, taking care to leave the skin intact. Chop the flesh into rough chunks and add to the pan of onion and garlic, along with the lime juice, chives and a good seasoning of salt and black pepper. Mix all the ingredients together well.
5 Place the avocado halves in a greased ovenproof dish and pile the mixture into them. Bake until heated through and beginning to brown on top: 10 minutes or so. Garnish with thin slices of lime and serve at once.

COURGETTES STUFFED WITH ALMONDS & RED PEPPER

You can serve these in a pool of yogurt and herb sauce or on a bed of Spiced rice (page 115), with a salad. Illustrated on page 25. Serves 4.

INGREDIENTS

*4 courgettes, halved lengthways
30ml (2 tbsps) olive oil
1 onion, chopped
2 red peppers, cored, deseeded and chopped
2 large cloves garlic, chopped
2 tsps finely chopped fresh thyme
45g (1½oz) flaked almonds, toasted briefly under a hot grill
salt and freshly ground black pepper*

PREPARATION

1 Preheat the oven to 180°C/350°F/gas 4.
2 Place the courgettes in a large saucepan, cover with boiling water and cook until just tender: 3 – 4 minutes. Drain and allow to cool.
3 Scoop out the seeds with a teaspoon, taking care to leave the skin intact. Chop the seeds and reserve to use in the stuffing. Place the courgette halves in a greased ovenproof dish.
4 Warm the oil in a saucepan over a moderate heat and add the onion and pepper. Cover and cook until they are soft: about 10 minutes. Add the garlic and cook for a further 2 minutes.
5 Remove from the heat and stir in the reserved courgette seeds along with the thyme and almonds. Season with salt and black pepper.
6 Spoon the filling into the courgette halves. Bake until heated through, about 15 minutes, and serve.

*Baby aubergines stuffed
with mushrooms and
pinenuts (below), and Herby
stuffed tomatoes (facing page)*

BABY AUBERGINES STUFFED WITH MUSHROOMS & NUTS

*These baby aubergines, illustrated above and
on page 24, serve 4, with three halves per person.*

INGREDIENTS

*6 baby aubergines, halved lengthways, stalks left on
15ml (1 tbsp) olive oil
1 medium-sized onion, chopped
1 clove garlic, chopped
125g (4oz) button mushrooms, chopped
2 tomatoes, chopped
1 tbsp chopped fresh flat-leaf parsley
30g (1oz) pinenuts
salt and freshly ground black pepper*

PREPARATION

1 Preheat the oven to 180°C/350°F/gas 4.
2 Place the aubergine halves in a saucepan, cover
with boiling water and cook until just tender:
3–4 minutes. Drain and allow to cool.
3 Scoop out the flesh with a teaspoon, leaving the
shells intact. Chop the flesh and reserve. Place the
shells in a greased ovenproof dish.
4 Warm the oil in a pan over a moderate heat,
add the onion, cover and cook for 5 minutes. Stir
in the aubergine flesh, garlic and mushrooms and
cook for 5 more minutes. Take off the heat, add
the tomato, parsley and most of the pinenuts
(reserving some for decoration) and season well.
5 Spoon the filling into the aubergines, sprinkle
with pinenuts, bake for 15 minutes, then serve.

HERBY STUFFED TOMATOES

Illustrated opposite and on page 25. Serves 4.

INGREDIENTS

1 shallot or small onion, finely chopped
3 tbsps chopped fresh flat-leaf parsley
1 tsp chopped fresh thyme
60g (2oz) dried breadcrumbs
30ml (2 tbsps) olive oil
4 beefsteak tomatoes
salt and freshly ground black pepper

PREPARATION

1 Preheat the oven to 180°C/350°F/gas 4.
(Alternatively, use a hot grill.)
2 In a bowl, mix together the onion, parsley,
thyme, breadcrumbs and olive oil. (If you have a
food processor, put unchopped onion, parsley and
thyme into it along with the breadcrumbs and
olive oil and chop finely to combine.)
3 Slice the tops off the tomatoes and reserve
them. Scoop out the seeds with a small teaspoon
to make a cavity for stuffing. You will not need the
inner flesh of the tomatoes for this recipe but you
can chop it and add it to a salad, soup or sauce.
4 Season the inside of the tomatoes with salt and
black pepper. Spoon in the stuffing, stand the
tomatoes in a greased ovenproof dish and replace
the tops. Cook in the oven or under a hot grill for
about 15 minutes, or until thoroughly heated
through but not collapsing. Serve warm or cold.

CREAM CHEESE MUSHROOMS

Illustrated on page 25. Serves 4.

INGREDIENTS

8 flat mushrooms
150g (5oz) full-fat cream cheese with garlic and herbs

PREPARATION

1 Preheat the grill to high.
2 Cut the stems of the mushrooms level with the
gills. Chop up the stems and put into a bowl with
the cream cheese and 2 tablespoons of hot water.
Mix well then spread over the mushroom gills.
Place the mushrooms in the grill pan.
3 Grill the mushrooms until the top is bubbling
and lightly browned and the mushrooms are
tender when pierced with a knife: about 10
minutes. Serve at once.

PEPPERS FILLED WITH GRILLED VEGETABLES

Illustrated on page 24. Serves 4.

INGREDIENTS

2 red and 2 yellow peppers
2 aubergines, cut into 1cm (½in) dice
1 large onion, sliced
olive oil, for brushing the vegetables
4 tomatoes, quartered
8 fresh basil leaves, lightly torn
15ml (1 tbsp) balsamic vinegar
salt and freshly ground black pepper

PREPARATION

1 Halve the peppers, cutting down through the
stem, then remove the seeds. Place the peppers,
cut-side down, in the grill pan and cook under a
hot grill for about 10 minutes, until the skins are
charred and blistered. Set aside.
2 Place the aubergine and onion in the grill pan,
brush with olive oil and cook under the hot grill
until tender and lightly browned: about 12
minutes. Turn the vegetables from time to time.
3 Add the tomatoes, turn all the vegetables again
and cook for another 3–5 minutes.
4 Put the grilled vegetables into a bowl and
sprinkle the basil, balsamic vinegar, salt and black
pepper over them. Toss gently.
5 Place the peppers cut-side up in a greased
ovenproof dish, removing or leaving on the papery
skin as you choose. Spoon the grilled vegetable
mixture into the cavities. Serve at once, at room
temperature, or reheat by covering with foil and
placing under a moderate grill or in the oven
(180°C/350°F/gas 4) for about 15 minutes.

PEPPERS & BABY SWEETCORN TERRINE

This delicate terrine has layers of peppers and baby corn separated by thin layers of egg custard. It needs slow cooking. Serves 6 as a starter, 4 as a main course.

INGREDIENTS

butter and dry grated Parmesan to coat the tin
3 free-range eggs
45ml (3 tbsps) single cream
3 tbsps freshly grated Parmesan
salt and freshly ground black pepper
500g (1lb) red peppers, grilled and peeled (page 144),
and cut lengthways into wide strips
250g (8oz) baby sweetcorn, cooked and drained,
or 400g (14oz) can baby sweetcorn, drained
175g (6oz) yellow peppers, grilled and peeled (page 144),
and cut lengthways into wide strips
sprigs of fresh basil, to garnish

PREPARATION

1 Preheat the oven to 150°C/300°F/gas 2. Line a 500g (1lb) loaf tin with a strip of nonstick paper to cover the base and narrow sides. Grease lightly with butter and dust with dry grated Parmesan.

2 Whisk together the eggs, cream, 2 tablespoons of the Parmesan and seasoning. Put 3 tablespoons of this mixture into the prepared tin.

3 Put one thin layer of red pepper into the tin and spoon a little egg mixture over it. Cover with another thin layer of red pepper, a little more egg, a third layer of red pepper, and a little more egg.

4 Make a layer of whole baby sweetcorn, laid lengthways, and spoon a little egg over it.

5 Make a thin layer of yellow pepper, followed by a little egg, another thin layer of yellow pepper, and a little more egg.

6 Repeat step 4 and then repeat step 3. Pour any remaining egg mixture over the top, and sprinkle with the remaining Parmesan.

7 Bake the terrine in a bain-marie (see page 147) until it is firm to the touch and a skewer inserted into the centre comes out clean: at least 1¼ hours. This is a delicate terrine that requires slightly slower cooking than the other terrines. Allow it to cool thoroughly before turning it out.

8 Loosen the terrine by slipping a knife down its two unlined sides. Invert the tin over a plate. Peel off the nonstick paper and slice the terrine carefully, sawing it with a sharp serrated knife. Serve with thin pesto sauce (page 123) and a garnish of basil.

TERRINE OF VEGETABLES IN A SPINACH COAT

Serves 6 as a starter, 4 as a main course.
Illustrated on page 12.

INGREDIENTS

butter and dry grated Parmesan to coat the tin
250g (8oz) large fresh spinach leaves, stems removed
60g (2oz) asparagus, trimmed to the length of the tin
175g (6oz) curd cheese
60g (2oz) freshly grated Parmesan cheese
2 tbsps chopped fresh chives
2 free-range eggs
salt and freshly ground black pepper
60g (2oz) sundried tomatoes, sliced
60g (2oz) artichoke hearts, preserved in oil or
canned and drained, sliced

PREPARATION

1 Preheat the oven to 160°C/325°F/gas 3. Line a 500g (1lb) loaf tin with a strip of nonstick paper to cover the base and narrow sides. Grease lightly with butter and dust with dry grated Parmesan.
2 Bring a saucepan of water to the boil. Drop in the spinach leaves and cook until tender: about 7 minutes. Drain well. Line the tin with the leaves so that they come up the sides and overhang the edges. Keep one or two leaves spare for the top.
3 Place the asparagus in a frying pan, cover with boiling water and cook until tender: 4–5 minutes. Drain and set aside.
4 Put the curd cheese into a bowl with the Parmesan and chives. Beat in the eggs until the mixture has a smooth creamy consistency, then season with salt and black pepper. Pour a little of the mixture into the base of the tin.
5 Build up the layers in the tin: asparagus spears laid lengthways, more curd cheese mixture, sundried tomato, more curd cheese, artichoke heart, the remainder of the curd cheese. Finally, fold the overhanging spinach over the top, and use the spare leaves to cover the top completely.
6 Bake the terrine in a bain-marie (see page 147) until it is firm to the touch and a skewer inserted into the centre comes out clean: about 1¼ hours. Allow it to cool thoroughly before turning it out.
7 Loosen the terrine by slipping a knife down its two unlined sides. Invert the tin over a plate to turn out the terrine. Peel off the nonstick paper and slice the terrine carefully using a sharp serrated knife in a sawing motion. Serve on individual plates with a sauce made from sundried tomatoes (page 121).

GREEN PEA, MINT & CAULIFLOWER TERRINE

Serves 6 as a starter, 4 as a main course.
Illustrated on page 13.

INGREDIENTS

butter and dry grated Parmesan to coat the tin
350g (12oz) frozen peas
175g (6oz) cauliflower florets
45g (1½oz) butter
3 free-range eggs
salt and freshly ground black pepper
2 tbsps lightly chopped fresh mint, plus a handful
of fresh mint leaves

PREPARATION

1 Preheat the oven to 160°C/325°F/gas 3. Line a 500g (1lb) loaf tin with a strip of nonstick paper to cover the base and narrow sides. Grease lightly with butter and dust with dry grated Parmesan.
2 Place the peas and the cauliflower in separate saucepans, cover with boiling water and cook until tender: 2–3 minutes in each case. Drain.
3 Put the peas into a food processor or blender with 30g (1oz) of the butter and 2 of the eggs and purée. Season with salt and black pepper and transfer to a bowl.
4 Put half the cauliflower florets into the cleaned food processor or blender with the remaining butter and egg. Work to a purée. Season with salt and black pepper and stir in the chopped mint.
5 Pour just under half of the pea purée into the prepared tin and cover with a good layer of mint leaves. Arrange the whole cauliflower florets on top and pour the puréed cauliflower over them. Cover with the remaining mint leaves in an even layer, and top with the rest of the pea purée.
6 Bake the terrine in a bain-marie (see page 147) until it is firm to the touch and a skewer inserted into the centre comes out clean: about 1¼ hours. Allow it to cool thoroughly before turning it out.
7 Loosen the terrine by slipping a knife down its two unlined sides. Invert the tin over a plate to turn out the terrine. Peel off the nonstick paper and slice the terrine carefully using a sharp serrated knife in a sawing motion. Serve on individual plates with a sauce of Greek yogurt (stir in a little saffron for colour) or warm homemade hollandaise (page 123).

LENTIL, CARROT & FENNEL TERRINE

Serves 6 as a starter, 4 as a main course.
Illustrated on page 13.

INGREDIENTS

butter and dry grated Parmesan to coat the tin
250g (8oz) fennel bulbs, sliced
125g (4oz) carrots, sliced
90g (3oz) red lentils
1 medium-sized onion, chopped
½ tsp turmeric
150ml (5fl oz) single cream
3 free-range eggs
pinch of ground cloves
salt and freshly ground black pepper
small bunch fresh flat-leaf parsley, chopped

PREPARATION

1 Preheat the oven to 160°C/325°F/gas 3. Line a 500g (1lb) loaf tin with a strip of nonstick paper to cover the base and narrow sides. Grease lightly with butter and dust with dry grated Parmesan.
2 Bring 3 saucepans of water to the boil. Cook the fennel and carrot separately until tender: 10–12 minutes. Drain. In the third saucepan, cook the lentils and onion until tender: about 15 minutes. Drain the lentil and onion mixture then stir the turmeric into it to boost its colour and flavour.
3 Put the lentil and onion mixture into a food processor or blender and work to a purée. Add the cream and eggs, along with the ground cloves and salt and black pepper to taste, and purée again. Transfer to a bowl.
4 Add the fennel, carrot and parsley to the lentil purée in the bowl and then, without mixing much, pour the mixture into the prepared tin. Tap the tin smartly several times to make sure the lentil purée runs into all the corners and fills it completely. The carrot, fennel and parsley will be randomly distributed in the terrine.
5 Bake the terrine in a bain-marie (see page 147) until it is firm to the touch and a skewer inserted into the centre comes out clean: about 1¼ hours. Allow it to cool thoroughly before turning it out.
6 Loosen the terrine by slipping a knife down its two unlined sides. Invert the tin over a plate to turn out the terrine. Peel off the nonstick paper and slice the terrine carefully using a sharp serrated knife in a sawing motion: the random distribution of the ingredients in the lentil mixture will be revealed. Serve on individual plates with red pepper sauce (page 120).

STRIPED VEGETABLE TERRINE

Serves 6 as a starter, 4 as a main course.
Illustrated on page 12.

INGREDIENTS

butter and dry grated Parmesan to coat the tin
250g (8oz) carrots, roughly chopped
250g (8oz) turnips, roughly chopped
300g (10oz) fresh podded or frozen broad beans
45g (1½oz) butter
45ml (3 tbsps) single cream
3 free-range eggs
salt and freshly ground black pepper
6 tbsps finely chopped fresh chervil

PREPARATION

1 Preheat the oven to 160°C/325°F/gas 3. Line a 500g (1lb) loaf tin with a strip of nonstick paper to cover the base and narrow sides. Grease lightly with butter and dust with dry grated Parmesan.
2 Bring 3 saucepans of water to the boil. Cook the carrot and turnip separately until tender: 10–12 minutes. Drain. In the third saucepan, cook the broad beans until tender: 5 minutes. Drain. When cool, pop off the bean skins using finger and thumb.
3 Put the carrots into a food processor or blender with a third of the butter, a third of the cream and 1 egg, and work to a purée. Season with salt and black pepper. Transfer to a bowl.
4 Repeat the process with the broad beans and the turnips, keeping the purées separate.
5 Pour the carrot purée into the prepared tin and sprinkle with half the chervil in an even layer. Repeat with the broad bean purée, cover with the rest of the chervil, then top with the turnip purée.
6 Bake the terrine in a bain-marie (see page 147) until it is firm to the touch and a skewer inserted into the centre comes out clean: about 1¼ hours. Allow it to cool thoroughly before turning it out.
7 Loosen the terrine by slipping a knife down its two unlined sides. Invert the tin over a plate to turn out the terrine. Peel off the nonstick paper and slice the terrine carefully using a sharp serrated knife in a sawing motion. Serve on individual plates with homemade fresh tomato sauce (page 121).

PUMPKIN, BROCCOLI & LEEK TERRINE

Serves 6 as a starter, 4 as a main course.
Illustrated on page 12.

INGREDIENTS

butter and dry grated Parmesan to coat the tin
400g (14oz) pumpkin, of which 250g (8oz) is diced
and 150g (6oz) is cut into thin, flat slices
250g (8oz) broccoli florets
4–6 thin leeks, the length of the loaf tin
45g (1½oz) butter
2 cloves garlic, chopped
3 free-range eggs
salt and freshly ground black pepper

PREPARATION

1 Preheat the oven to 160°C/325°F/gas 3. Line a 500g (1lb) loaf tin with a strip of nonstick paper to cover the base and narrow sides. Grease lightly with butter and dust with dry grated Parmesan.
2 Bring 3 saucepans of water to the boil. Cook the pumpkin, broccoli and whole leeks separately until tender. test with the point of a knife. Drain.
3 Melt the butter in a small saucepan, add the garlic and fry for 1–2 minutes over a moderate heat until the garlic is golden but not browned.
4 Put the garlic with its butter into the food processor or blender, along with the *diced* pumpkin, eggs, and salt and black pepper to taste. Work to a purée.
5 Put a thin layer of the purée into the prepared tin, cover with the broccoli florets in an even layer, and cover again with a layer of the purée.
6 Continue to fill up the tin in layers: next use half of the pumpkin slices, then a little more purée, the leeks, enough purée to hold the leeks in place, the remaining pumpkin slices, and finally the remaining purée.
7 Bake the terrine in a bain-marie (see page 147) until it is firm to the touch and a skewer inserted into the centre comes out clean: about 1¼ hours. Allow it to cool thoroughly before turning it out.
8 Loosen the terrine by slipping a knife down its two unlined sides. Invert the tin over a plate to turn out the terrine. Peel off the nonstick paper and slice the terrine carefully using a sharp serrated knife in a sawing motion. Serve on individual plates with green pepper sauce (page 120) or a little mayonnaise (page 122) mixed into Greek yogurt.

BLUE CHEESE, LEEK & WATERCRESS TERRINE

This is good hot or cold. Served hot it is lovely as part of a Christmas meal, especially accompanied by red wine sauce (page 121). Serves 6 as a starter, 4 as a main course.

INGREDIENTS

butter and dry grated Parmesan to coat the tin
30g (1oz) butter
1 medium-sized onion, chopped
500g (1lb) trimmed leeks, sliced
60g (2oz) watercress, roughly chopped, with a few
sprigs reserved for garnishing
3 free-range eggs, beaten
125g (4oz) blue cheese, crumbled
freshly ground black pepper

PREPARATION

1 Preheat the oven to 160°C/325°F/gas 3. Line a 500g (1lb) loaf tin with a strip of nonstick paper to cover the base and narrow sides. Grease lightly with butter and dust with dry grated Parmesan.
2 Melt the butter in a medium large saucepan over a moderate heat, add the onion, cover and cook until tender: about 5 minutes.
3 Add the leeks and watercress to the pan and cook, uncovered, until they are tender and any liquid has evaporated: 5–10 minutes. Remove from the heat and allow to cool slightly.
4 Mix the eggs and blue cheese into the mixture. Stir well to combine the ingredients and season with black pepper (no salt because blue cheese is already high in salt). Pour into the prepared tin.
5 Bake the terrine in a bain-marie (see page 147) until it is firm to the touch and a skewer inserted into the centre comes out clean: about 1¼ hours. Allow it to cool thoroughly before turning it out.
6 Loosen the terrine by slipping a knife down its two unlined sides. Invert the tin over a plate to turn out the terrine. Peel off the nonstick paper. To serve warm, cover the turned-out terrine in foil and place in a moderate oven (160°C/325°F/gas 4) for around 15 minutes. Slice the terrine carefully using a sharp serrated knife in a sawing motion. Serve, warm or cold, on individual plates with red wine sauce (page 121).

CASHEW NUT KORMA

Creamy and lightly spiced, this is delicious served with plain boiled rice (page 152). Like many casseroles and spiced dishes, it benefits from being made in advance because the flavours get a chance to develop and blend; it also reheats well. Serves 4.

INGREDIENTS

75g (3oz) creamed coconut, cut into flakes
30ml (2 tbsps) sunflower oil
2 medium-sized onions, chopped
2 fresh green chillies, deseeded and finely sliced
2 cloves garlic, chopped
½ tsp ground cumin
½ tsp turmeric
½ tsp ground coriander
125g (4oz) cashew nuts, puréed in a blender or finely ground in a mouli
salt and freshly ground black pepper
250g (8oz) long-grain white or brown rice
½ medium-sized cauliflower, divided into florets
125g (4oz) okra, trimmed
125g (4oz) courgettes, sliced
125g (4oz) frozen peas
2−4 tbsps chopped fresh coriander

PREPARATION

1 Put the coconut into a bowl and cover with 450ml (15fl oz) boiling water. Stir, then leave to melt completely.

2 Meanwhile, warm the oil in a large saucepan over a moderate heat, add the onion, cover and cook until tender: 5−7 minutes.

3 Add the chillies, garlic and spices, stir well and cook for a further 1−2 minutes. Remove from the heat and set aside.

4 Stir the cashew nuts into the bowl containing the coconut. Add this mixture to the onion and flavourings in the pan and season with salt and black pepper. Cover and set aside once more.

You can prepare ahead to this point. The coconut and cashew mixture keeps for up to 24 hours in a covered container in the refrigerator.

5 Cook the rice (see page 152). When the rice is almost ready, cook the vegetables. Pour 1cm (½in) of boiling water into a large saucepan, add the cauliflower and okra, cover and half-boil, half-steam for 1 minute. Add the courgettes, cover again and cook for 3 more minutes. Drain.

6 Stir the vegetables into the creamy cashew nut mixture along with the frozen peas. Warm through over a gentle heat. Check the seasoning and serve, sprinkled with coriander, with the rice.

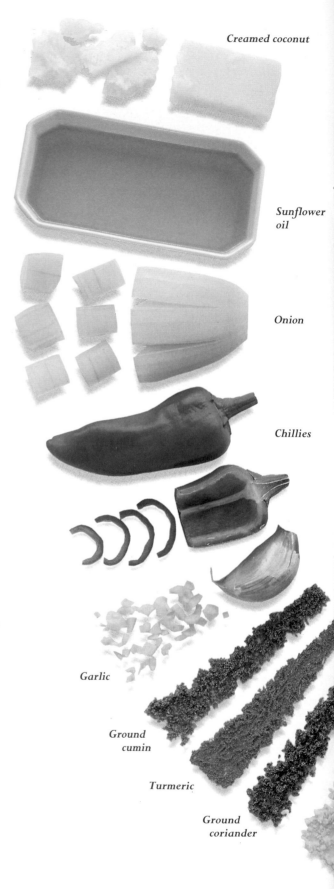

Creamed coconut

Sunflower oil

Onion

Chillies

Garlic

Ground cumin

Turmeric

Ground coriander

Cashew nuts

Fresh coriander

Salt   Black
       pepper White
               rice   Cauliflower   Okra   Courgette   Peas

CHINESE-STYLE STIR-FRY WITH MARINATED TOFU

Serve this Chinese-style stir-fry with plain boiled rice and provide some extra soy sauce in small bowls; for 4.

INGREDIENTS

MARINATED TOFU
300g (10oz) firm tofu, cut into 1cm (½in) cubes
45ml (3 tbsps) soy sauce
15ml (1 tbsp) sesame oil
1 clove garlic, chopped

THE STIR-FRY
125g (4oz) carrots
250g (8oz) beansprouts
125g (4oz) baby sweetcorn
125g (4oz) mangetout
small bunch of spring onions
200g (7oz) can water chestnuts
200g (7oz) can bamboo shoots
125g (4oz) straw mushrooms (from a jar or can)
or 125g (4oz) button mushrooms
1 tbsp cornflour
walnut-sized piece of fresh ginger, unpeeled, grated
pinch of five-spice powder
15ml (1 tbsp) medium sherry
60ml (4 tbsps) soy sauce
30ml (2 tbsps) groundnut oil

PREPARATION

1 First prepare the tofu, which needs to marinate for around an hour. Put it into a shallow bowl that will fit under the grill, sprinkle with the soy sauce, sesame oil and garlic and stir gently so that all the tofu is coated. Cover and set aside.

2 Prepare the vegetables. Slice the carrots very thinly at an angle. Rinse and drain the beansprouts and sweetcorn. Trim the mangetout and spring onions. Drain the water chestnuts, bamboo shoots and straw mushrooms. Slice any fresh mushrooms.

3 In a small bowl, mix the cornflour, ginger, five-spice powder, sherry and soy into a smooth paste.

4 Just before you want to serve the stir-fry, place the marinated tofu under a hot grill. Turn the pieces of tofu until they are crisp on all sides and heated through: 3–4 minutes.

5 Meanwhile, pour the groundnut oil into a wok or a large frying pan and place over a high heat.

6 When the oil is smoking hot, put in all the vegetables and stir-fry until evenly heated through but still crisp: about 1–2 minutes.

7 Stir the cornflour mixture and add it to the wok or pan. Stir-fry over the heat for another minute until thickened. Add the tofu, and serve at once.

SUMMER STIR-FRY WITH TOASTED ALMONDS

Summer is the perfect time for a stir-fry: the tender young vegetables and fresh herbs are ideal ingredients. Serves 4.

INGREDIENTS

juice and rind of 1 lemon
250g (8oz) asparagus tips
250g (8oz) courgettes
250g (8oz) baby carrots
250g (8oz) broccoli
250g (8oz) mangetout
250g (8oz) green beans
30ml (2 tbsps) groundnut oil
4 tbsps chopped flat-leaf parsley
salt and freshly ground black pepper
100g (3½oz) flaked almonds, toasted briefly under a hot grill

PREPARATION

1 Remove the pith from the lemon rind and cut the rind into thin strips. Set rind and juice aside.

2 Prepare the vegetables. Trim the asparagus tips if necessary. Cut the courgettes into matchsticks. Slice the baby carrots at an angle. Cut the broccoli into florets. Trim the mangetout and green beans.

3 Pour the groundnut oil into a wok or a large frying pan and place over a high heat.

4 When the oil is smoking hot, put in all the vegetables and stir-fry until evenly heated through but still crisp: about 1–2 minutes.

5 Add the lemon rind, 2 tablespoons of lemon juice, the parsley, salt and black pepper and stir-fry for another minute. Serve at once, with almonds sprinkled over the top.

VARIATION

To 60g (2oz) of flaked almonds, add 60g (2oz) of pumpkin and sunflower seeds. Spread out in a grill pan, sprinkle with 60ml (4 tbsps) of soy sauce, and crisp under a hot grill: 5–10 minutes, shaking the pan occasionally so they cook evenly. Set aside to cool. Sprinkle over the stir-fry.

STIR-FRY WITH GOMASIO

Gomasio is a mixture of sesame seeds and salt, toasted and ground to a powder as a piquant topping for stir-fried vegetables. It can be made at home and stored in an airtight container for up to a week. As always, you can vary the vegetables used for the stir-fry, according to your taste and what is available. Serves 4.

INGREDIENTS

THE GOMASIO
6 tbsps sesame seeds
1½ tsps sea salt

THE STIR-FRY
2 bunches of spring onions
350g (12oz) daikon or turnip
350g (12oz) carrots
350g (12oz) mangetout
2 bunches of radishes
walnut-sized piece of fresh ginger
1 clove garlic
30ml (2 tbsps) groundnut oil
60ml (4 tbsps) soy sauce

PREPARATION

1 First make the gomasio. Put the sesame seeds and salt into a dry frying pan and stir over a high heat until the seeds smell toasted, turn slightly darker and start to pop: 1–2 minutes. Remove from the heat and leave to cool, then make into a powder in an electric coffee grinder or a blender. Put in a small bowl for serving.

2 Prepare the vegetables. Trim the spring onions or make into tassels as shown on page 145. Cut the daikon or turnip into matchsticks. Dice the carrots. Trim the mangetout. Slice the radishes. Grate the ginger and chop the garlic.

3 Pour the groundnut oil into a wok or a large frying pan and place over a high heat.

4 When the oil is smoking hot, put in all the vegetables along with the ginger and garlic and stir-fry until evenly heated through but still crisp: about 1–2 minutes.

5 Add the soy sauce and stir-fry for another minute. Serve at once, with the gomasio in a small bowl or sprinkled over the stir-fry.

Parmigiana di Melanzane

Traditionally, this southern Italian aubergine pie is made with fried aubergines, which can make the dish rather oily, so I boil or steam the slices of aubergine instead. With the richness of the cheeses and the oil in the tomato sauce, I find the result just right. Serve with bread, a leafy salad and some red wine. For 4.

INGREDIENTS

750g (1½lb) aubergines, thinly sliced
30ml (2 tbsps) olive oil
2 medium-sized onions, chopped
2 cloves garlic, chopped
2 x 400g (14oz) cans whole peeled tomatoes, coarsely chopped, with juice
salt and freshly ground black pepper
250g (8oz) mozzarella cheese, sliced
60g (2oz) freshly grated Parmesan cheese

PREPARATION

1 Preheat the oven to 200°C/400°F/gas 6.
2 Steam or boil the aubergines until just tender. To steam them you may need to do them in more than one batch, depending on the size of the steamer, but they take only a few minutes.
3 Meanwhile, warm the oil in a medium-large saucepan over a moderate heat, add the onion, cover and cook for 5 minutes. Add the garlic and cook for another minute.
4 Pour in the tomatoes together with their juice and cook, uncovered, until the liquid evaporates and the mixture has reduced: about 15 minutes. Season with salt and black pepper. This is the tomato sauce.
5 Put a layer of aubergine slices into a shallow, lightly greased, ovenproof dish. Cover with slices of mozzarella and a little tomato sauce. Repeat the layers until the ingredients have been used, ending with a layer of tomato sauce. Sprinkle the Parmesan cheese over the top.
6 Bake, uncovered, in the preheated oven until golden brown and bubbling: 25–30 minutes. Serve at once.

VARIATIONS

This aubergine pie is best made with good mozzarella cheese packed in water. Alternatives would be another Italian cheese, such as Bel Paese, or – totally inauthentic but still delicious – slices of Brie or Camembert. For a complete change, you can make a version of this dish using slices of cooked potato instead of half, or all, of the aubergine. It ceases then to be Parmigiana di melanzane but is delicious and filling all the same.

Courgette & Tomato Gratin

This is one of my favourite summer dishes. With new potatoes and salad, it makes a light meal. Serves 4 as a first course, 2 as a main course.

INGREDIENTS

30g (1oz) butter
45ml (3 tbsps) olive oil
750g (1½lb) courgettes, thinly sliced
1 medium-sized onion, chopped
1 clove garlic, chopped
500g (1lb) fresh tomatoes, peeled and roughly chopped
salt and freshly ground black pepper
30g (1oz) soft fresh breadcrumbs

PREPARATION

1 Preheat the oven to 200°C/400°F/gas 6.
2 Melt the butter with 1 tablespoon of the oil in a large saucepan over a moderate heat, add the courgettes, cover and cook until just tender to the point of a knife: 5–7 minutes. You may need to cook the courgettes in two batches, depending on the size of the pan.
3 Meanwhile, warm the rest of the oil in a medium-large saucepan over a moderate heat, add the onion, cover and cook for 5 minutes. Add the garlic and cook for another minute.
4 Reduce the heat under the onions, add the tomatoes, cover and cook until they have collapsed and any water they give off has evaporated: about 15 minutes. Season well with salt and black pepper. This is the tomato sauce.
5 Stir the courgettes into the tomato sauce and pour into a shallow, lightly greased, ovenproof dish. Make the top level, sprinkle it with breadcrumbs and dot with the remaining butter.
6 Bake, uncovered, in the preheated oven until the top is golden brown and crisp: 25–30 minutes. Serve at once.

VARIATIONS

LEEK GRATIN is the winter version. Replace the courgettes with the same weight of trimmed leeks. Slice the leeks thinly and cook gently in the butter and oil until tender: about 15 minutes. Add to the tomato sauce and continue as above.
PARSNIP, POTATO OR KOHLRABI GRATIN Replace the courgettes with the same weight of parsnips, potatoes or kohlrabi, cut into slices about 5mm (¼in) thick and steamed or boiled until just tender. Arrange the vegetables in the casserole dish in layers, spreading each layer with the tomato sauce.

ROASTED MEDITERRANEAN VEGETABLES

This is one of the easiest vegetable dishes to prepare and one of the most versatile and delicious. The amount of garlic may seem large — a whole bulb rather than just a clove or two — but when roasted it becomes very mild in flavour. It doesn't need peeling before cooking or serving; just pop the cloves of garlic out of their skins at the table and eat the creamy insides. Serves 4, with a substantial plateful each.

INGREDIENTS

3 fennel bulbs
3 red peppers
3 aubergines
3 red onions
olive oil
1 garlic bulb
45ml (3 tbsps) balsamic vinegar
fresh basil leaves, to taste
salt and freshly ground black pepper

PREPARATION

1 Preheat the oven to 230°C/450°F/gas 8.
2 Trim the fennel bulbs, removing any of the outer layers which seem too tough. Slice through each bulb from top to bottom, cutting it first into halves, then into quarters, then eighths. Each segment will be kept together by its share of the root end. Steam or parboil the fennel for about 8 minutes, or until it is just tender without being soggy. Drain and dry well with kitchen paper.
3 Cut the peppers into chunks, discarding the seeds and core. Don't peel them; it is easy to scoop the tender sweet flesh away from the skin after they are roasted, and some people like to eat the roasted skin.
4 Trim the aubergines and cut them into chunks.
5 Peel the onions and slice them into eighths in the same way as the fennel.
6 Brush all these vegetables with olive oil, put them into a roasting tin and roast for 20 minutes.
7 Remove the roasting tin from the oven. Break the garlic into cloves and add these, unpeeled, to the tin, turning the other vegetables as necessary to allow them to roast evenly. Return the vegetables to the oven, reduce the heat to 180°C/350°F/gas 4, and roast until tender and browned in places: about 15–20 minutes more.
8 Transfer to a serving dish, sprinkle with the vinegar and some torn basil leaves and season with salt and black pepper. Serve hot or warm.

ROASTED ROOT VEGETABLES

A mixture of different root vegetables, roasted together, makes a warming winter dish. Vary the vegetables according to what is available, and serve with a nutritious dipping sauce such as hummus (page 59) if desired. The quantities given here serve 4, with a substantial plateful each.

INGREDIENTS

750g (1½lb) celeriac
750g (1½lb) parsnips
750g (1½lb) carrots
750g (1½lb) potatoes
90ml (6 tbsps) olive or groundnut oil
crunchy sea salt

PREPARATION

1 Preheat the oven to 230°C/450°F/gas 8.
2 Once the oven is hot, pour the oil into two roasting tins and place them in the oven to heat up.
3 Prepare the vegetables as necessary and cut them into even-sized pieces.
4 Put the vegetables into the hot oil, spooning oil over them so that they are coated all over, then roast for 20 minutes.
5 Reduce the heat to 180°C/350°F/gas 4. Turn the vegetables to allow them to cook evenly, then continue to roast until crisp outside and tender inside: about 15–20 minutes more.
6 Remove from the oven, blot on kitchen paper, sprinkle with sea salt and serve immediately.

VEGETABLE TEMPURA

This Japanese-inspired dish of vegetables in crisp, light batter makes a delicious treat. Many different vegetables can be used: cut into small pieces for quick cooking, or parboil first, which is the best way to prepare cauliflower and broccoli florets, for example. Serve the tempura the minute they are done, with the dipping sauce on the side. As a main course, serve with plain boiled rice. Serves 4 as a first course, 2 as a main course.

INGREDIENTS

1 medium-sized carrot, cut into matchsticks
1 red onion, thinly sliced
125g (4oz) mangetout, trimmed
125g (4oz) shiitake mushrooms, thinly sliced
THE DIPPING SAUCE
walnut-sized piece of fresh ginger, unpeeled, grated
30ml (2 tbsps) mirin (sweet rice wine) **or** *1½ tsps clear honey dissolved in 15ml (1 tbsp) hot water*
45ml (3 tbsps) soy sauce
THE BATTER
made at the last minute, from 1 egg, broken into
125g (4oz) plain flour sifted with salt, with
125ml (4fl oz) tepid water stirred in
FOR FRYING
oil such as groundnut

PREPARATION

1 Have all the prepared vegetables to hand.
2 Mix together the ingredients for the dipping sauce. Pour into individual bowls.
3 The batter, which does not need to stand, can be made at the last minute. Break the egg into the flour and salt and mix lightly with a fork. Add 125ml (4fl oz) tepid water and stir to make a batter – it should not be completely smooth.
4 Pour about 8cm (3in) of oil into a large saucepan or deep-frier and place over a high heat.
5 When the oil reaches a temperature of 180°C/350°F – when bubbles form on a wooden chopstick or the handle of a wooden spoon stirred into it – dip three or four pieces of vegetable into the batter and drop them into the oil.
6 Fry the tempura until crisp underneath (about 1 minute), then turn them over with a slotted spoon and fry the other side for 1 minute. Drain on kitchen paper, but don't cover them or they will lose their crispness.
7 Quickly skim any bits from the oil using a slotted spoon and put in another small batch of freshly battered vegetables. Continue until they are all fried, and serve at once with the dipping sauce.

Shiitake mushrooms

Mangetout

Red onion

Carrot

Soy sauce

Fresh ginger

Mirin

Batter

Groundnut oil

CREPE GATEAU

Crêpes layered with a rich-tasting aubergine mixture and topped with creamy béchamel sauce and Parmesan cheese, garnished with bright red cherry tomatoes and sprigs of fresh oregano: this makes a wonderful main course that looks dramatic when brought to the table. Slice it into thick wedges like a cake. Serves 4 to 6.

INGREDIENTS

THE CREPES
1 quantity of crêpe batter (page 149)
olive oil for frying the crêpes

THE FILLING
60ml (4 tbsps) olive oil
2 large onions, chopped
4 large cloves garlic, chopped
1.5kg (3lb) aubergines, finely diced
60g (2oz) plain flour
*2 x 400g (14oz) cans whole peeled tomatoes,
coarsely chopped, with juice*
300ml (½ pint) red wine
250g (8oz) button mushrooms, sliced
2 tbsps chopped fresh oregano
salt and freshly ground black pepper

THE TOPPING
450ml (¾ pint) freshly made béchamel sauce (page 148)
150ml (5fl oz) single cream
freshly grated nutmeg
30–60g (1–2oz) freshly grated Parmesan cheese
cherry tomatoes and sprigs of oregano, to garnish

PREPARATION

THE CREPES
1 Make the batter as described and place it next to the hob with a ladle.
2 Brush a frying pan measuring about 20cm/8in across the base (or a slightly larger than standard crêpe pan) with olive oil and place over a high heat. Once the olive oil is hot enough to sizzle when a drop of water is dropped into it, take the pan off the heat and, using the ladle, pour in enough batter to coat the base. Return to the heat and let the crêpe cook until the top is set and lightly browned: about 1 minute. Flip it over.
3 Cook the second side until lightly browned: just a few seconds. Lift the crêpe out of the pan on to a piece of foil. Reheat the pan – you won't need to regrease it every time – and make five more crêpes in the same way, stacking them up. Cover with foil until you need them.

 The crêpes can be prepared ahead of time. Wrap in foil and keep in the refrigerator for up to 3 days, or in the freezer for up to 3 months.

THE FILLING
1 Warm 45ml (3 tbsps) of the oil in a large saucepan over a moderate heat, add the onions and garlic, cover and cook for 5 minutes. Then stir in the aubergine, cover and cook until tender: 15–20 minutes. Stir from time to time.
2 Sprinkle the flour on to the aubergine, stir over the heat for another minute or two, then pour in the tomatoes with their juice and the red wine. Continue to stir over the heat until the mixture has thickened, then reduce the heat, cover and leave for 8–10 minutes to cook the flour. Remove from the heat.
3 In another pan, warm the remaining tablespoon of oil over a moderate heat, add the mushrooms and fry until tender and lightly browned: 3–5 minutes. Drain the mushrooms of any liquid and add them to the aubergine mixture. Stir in the oregano and season with salt and black pepper.

TO ASSEMBLE AND BAKE
1 Preheat the oven to 200°C/400°F/gas 6. Place one of the crêpes (thawed if necessary) on a large heatproof plate. Cover it evenly with a fifth of the aubergine mixture (it should make a thick layer). Put another crêpe on top, cover with another fifth of the aubergine mixture, and so on, finishing with a crêpe on top.
2 Gently warm the béchamel sauce, then stir in the cream. Check the seasoning, adding some nutmeg. Pour enough sauce over the crêpe gâteau to cover the top and run attractively down the sides. The rest can be poured into a jug to be served alongside the dish.
3 Sprinkle the Parmesan on top of the gâteau and bake, uncovered, until it is heated right through and golden brown on top: about 20 minutes. Garnish with cherry tomatoes and sprigs of oregano and serve immediately.

MUSTARD SEED CREPES WITH SPICED VEGETABLE FILLING

Mustard seeds give these crêpes a crunchy texture and a bit of a kick but the crêpes are not hot. The filling, too, is spicy but mild. The recipe has no exotic source as far as I am aware; it was just an idea I had one day. Mango chutney and a sliced tomato and onion salad go well with the crêpes. Serves 4 to 6.

INGREDIENTS

THE CREPES

1 quantity of crêpe batter (page 149)
2 tbsps mustard seeds
olive oil for frying the crêpes

THE FILLING

30ml (2 tbsps) olive oil
1 large onion, chopped
2 cloves garlic, chopped
½ tsp turmeric
2 tsps cumin seeds
500g (1lb) potatoes, peeled and diced
250g (8oz) fresh young spinach leaves
salt and freshly ground black pepper

PREPARATION

THE CREPES

1 Preheat the oven to 180°C/350°F/gas 4 so that you can keep the crêpes warm as they are done (unless you are preparing them in advance to eat later). Make the batter as described, stir in the mustard seeds, and place the batter next to the hob with a ladle. Stir the batter each time you make a crêpe to keep the seeds well distributed.

2 Brush a crêpe pan (or a small frying pan measuring about 15cm/6in across the base) with olive oil and place over a high heat. Once the olive oil is hot enough to sizzle when a drop of water is flicked into it, take the pan off the heat and, using the ladle, pour in enough batter to coat the base. Return to the heat and let the crêpe cook until the top is set and lightly browned: about 1 minute. Flip it over.

3 Cook the second side until lightly browned: just a few seconds. Lift the crêpe out of the pan on to a piece of foil. Reheat the pan – you won't need to regrease it every time – and make the rest of the crêpes in the same way, stacking them up. Cover with foil until you need them.

 The crêpes can be prepared ahead of time. Wrap in foil and keep in the refrigerator for up to 3 days, or in the freezer for up to 3 months.

THE FILLING

1 Warm the oil in a large saucepan over a moderate heat, add the onion and fry for 5 minutes. Stir in the garlic and spices and fry, stirring, for 1–2 minutes.

2 Stir in the potatoes, coating well with the oil and spices. Then add the spinach and cook, stirring, until the spinach and potatoes are tender: about 10–12 minutes. Season to taste.

3 Preheat the oven to 180°C/350°F/gas 4.

4 Spread the filling thinly over each crêpe (thawed if necessary), roll them up and place them side by side in a lightly greased, shallow casserole dish. Cover with foil.

5 Reheat gently for about 20 minutes, and serve.

VEGETABLE SIDE DISHES

Creamy potato gratins, vegetable ribbons with herbs, warm and spicy red cabbage, puréed celeriac, buttered leeks: vegetables are flavoursome, health-giving and highly adaptable ingredients. Vegetarian meals are often loosely structured, and a range of simple, lightly cooked vegetable side dishes can accompany a more elaborate main dish or even play the starring role in a meal. Whatever the occasion, aim for contrasting colours and textures in the vegetables.

GRATIN DAUPHINOIS

This dish adds a touch of luxury to any meal – and it couldn't be easier to make. Serves 4.

INGREDIENTS

750g (1½lb) potatoes, peeled
45g (1½oz) butter
1 – 2 cloves garlic, chopped
freshly grated nutmeg, salt, freshly ground black pepper
150ml (5fl oz) double cream
300ml (½ pint) milk

PREPARATION

1 Preheat the oven to 150°C/300°F/gas 2.
2 Cut the potatoes into the thinnest slices possible; use a mandoline or a food processor with a slicing disc if you have one. Rinse the potatoes in a bowl of water then place in a colander to drain.
3 Grease a casserole dish with half the butter. Scatter the garlic over the base of the dish, then put in the potatoes in even layers, seasoning with nutmeg, salt and pepper as you go. Cover with the cream and milk and dot with the rest of the butter.
4 Bake, uncovered, until the potatoes are tender when pierced with the point of a knife and the top layer is golden and crisp: 1½ – 2 hours.

WILD MUSHROOM GRATIN DAUPHINOIS

Serves 4.

INGREDIENTS

20g (⅔oz) packet dried wild mushrooms
750g (1½lb) potatoes, peeled
45g (1½oz) butter
1 – 2 cloves garlic, chopped
salt and freshly ground black pepper
150ml (5fl oz) double cream
300ml (½ pint) milk

PREPARATION

1 Preheat the oven to 150°C/300°F/gas 2.
2 Put the mushrooms in a small bowl, cover with boiling water and leave to soak for a few minutes. Meanwhile, follow step 2 for Gratin dauphinois.
3 Drain and chop the reconstituted mushrooms.
4 Grease a casserole dish with half the butter and scatter the garlic into the dish. Make a layer of potato, then of mushroom, season with salt and pepper, and continue until the ingredients are used up, finishing with potatoes. Cover with the cream and milk and dot with the rest of the butter.
5 Follow step 4 for Gratin dauphinois.

TOMATO GRATIN DAUPHINOIS

Serves 4.

INGREDIENTS

750g (1½lb) potatoes, peeled
60ml (4 tbsps) olive oil
1 clove garlic, chopped
750g (1½lb) tomatoes, peeled and chopped
salt and freshly ground black pepper
fresh basil leaves, roughly torn, to taste

PREPARATION

1 Follow steps 1 and 2 for Gratin dauphinois.
2 Grease a casserole dish with half the oil and scatter the garlic into the dish. Make a layer of potato, then of tomato, season with salt and black pepper, and continue until all the ingredients are used up, finishing with a layer of potatoes. Pour the remaining oil on top.
3 Follow step 4 for Gratin dauphinois. Serve garnished with fresh basil.

FANTAIL ROAST POTATOES

An attractive variation on roast potatoes. You can follow
steps 1 and 2 ahead of time, and put the potatoes in the
hot oven later. To serve 4, use 1kg (2lb) of potatoes
and 60g (2oz) of melted butter.

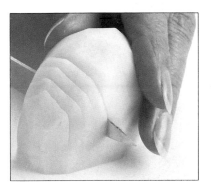

*1 Peel and halve the potatoes. Cut fine
slits in the top of each one, without
going through the base, so the potato
stays intact.*

*2 Parboil the potatoes for 5 minutes.
Drain. Stand them on a greased
baking sheet and brush all over with
melted butter.*

*3 Preheat the oven to 200°C / 400°F /
gas 6. Bake the potatoes until
golden and crisp outside, and tender
inside: 40–60 minutes. Serve at once.*

ROSTI WITH SAGE

*Crisp, fragrant and "moreish", rosti is best made in one
big round, which you cut into wedges to serve. Instead of
sage, try rosemary or thyme, or even 1 to 2 tablespoons
of crushed juniper berries. Serves 4.*

INGREDIENTS

*1kg (2lb) potatoes, skins left on
salt
2 tbsps chopped fresh sage
olive or sunflower oil for frying*

PREPARATION

1 Place the potatoes in a saucepan, cover with
cold water, bring to the boil and cook for about 5
minutes, or until they are just tender to the point
of a knife. Drain and leave to cool.
2 Slip the skins off the potatoes using a small
sharp knife and your fingers. Grate the potatoes
coarsely, season with salt and add the herbs.
3 Pour enough oil into a large frying pan to cover
the base, and place over a moderate heat. Once
the oil is hot, put in the potatoes, pressing down
with a spatula to make one big round. Fry until
crisp and brown underneath: about 8 minutes. Tip
the rosti out on to a plate, cooked side up, then
slide it back into the pan to cook the second side.
4 Continue to cook until the second side is
browned and crisp, then drain on kitchen paper
and serve at once.

POTATO PANCAKES

*This is a quick, simple and delicious way to prepare
potatoes. They make a good snack; children
in particular love to eat them, especially if served with
tomato ketchup and baked beans. Serves 4.*

INGREDIENTS

*500g (1lb) potatoes, peeled
1 small onion
1 tbsp plain flour
2 eggs, beaten
salt and freshly ground black pepper
olive or sunflower oil for frying*

PREPARATION

1 Grate the raw potatoes coarsely. Rinse the
grated potato at once, then drain it, pat dry, and
transfer to a bowl.
2 Grate the onion over the potato. Sprinkle with
the flour, pour in the eggs and season with salt and
black pepper. Beat into a lumpy batter.
3 Pour enough oil into a frying pan to cover the
base, and place over a moderate heat. Once the oil
is hot, drop in tablespoonfuls of potato mixture,
flattening them with the back of the spoon. Fry
the pancakes until crisp and brown underneath:
about 3 minutes. Turn them over and cook the
other side. The potato inside will be tender by the
time both sides are crisp.
4 Serve at once, or keep warm in the oven.

TAGLIATELLE OF CABBAGE

*Cabbage is cut into long strands to resemble
tagliatelle, then tossed in butter and an aromatic spice.
This dish is better made with a soft whitish-green
cabbage than with a very hard white one. Serves 4.*

INGREDIENTS

*500–750g (1–1½lb) white cabbage
15g (½oz) butter
freshly grated nutmeg, whole caraway seeds **or**
powdered cinnamon
salt and freshly ground black pepper*

PREPARATION

1 Remove and discard the tough central stem
of the cabbage then slice the leaves into long thin
strands to resemble tagliatelle. You can use either
a knife or a swivel-bladed peeler to do this.
2 Pour 1cm (½in) of boiling water into a saucepan
and add the cabbage. Cover the pan and half-boil,
half-steam the cabbage over a moderate heat until
just tender: 5–7 minutes. (Most of the cabbage
will be out of the water: it steams rather than
boils, retaining flavour and nutrients.) Drain.
3 Transfer the vegetable to a bowl and add the
butter, along with the spice of your choice and salt
and pepper to taste. Toss well, and serve at once.

CARROT & COURGETTE RIBBONS WITH PESTO

*The vegetables are sliced into long strands and mixed
with fragrant pesto for this pretty, summery dish.
Illustrated on page 84. Serves 4.*

INGREDIENTS

*250g (8oz) large carrots, scraped and trimmed
250g (8oz) medium-sized or large courgettes, trimmed
30ml (2 tbsps) pesto (for homemade, see page 123)
salt and freshly ground black pepper*

PREPARATION

1 Cut the carrots and courgettes into long, fine
strands or ribbons by drawing a swivel-bladed
peeler down the length of them.
2 Pour 1cm (½in) of boiling water into a saucepan
and add the carrots. Cover the pan and half-boil,
half-steam the carrots over a moderate heat for
2–3 minutes. Add the courgettes and cook for
1–2 minutes longer. (Courgettes cook quickly;
don't let them become waterlogged.) Drain.
3 Transfer the vegetables to a bowl, add the pesto
and a little seasoning, mix well and serve at once.

JULIENNE OF KOHLRABI

*Kohlrabi is a root vegetable rather like turnip, with a
delicate flavour and a pleasantly crunchy texture. Its
smooth skin is pale green or purple. Serves 4.*

INGREDIENTS

*750g (1½lb) kohlrabi
15g (½oz) butter
salt and freshly ground black pepper*

PREPARATION

1 Peel the kohlrabi thinly; I find a swivel-bladed
peeler best for this. Then cut the flesh into
julienne strips (see page 145).
2 Pour 1cm (½in) of boiling water into a saucepan
and add the kohlrabi. Cover the pan and half-boil,
half-steam the kohlrabi over a moderate heat until
just tender: about 2 minutes. Drain.
3 Transfer the kohlrabi to a bowl and add the
butter and salt and black pepper to taste. Toss
well, and serve at once.

JULIENNE OF BEETROOT

*A quick and delicious way to serve beetroot. Use
ready-cooked beetroot if you wish, but choose ones that
have been prepared without vinegar. Serves 4.*

INGREDIENTS

*750g (1½lb) raw beetroot
juice and peel of 1 orange
15g (½oz) butter
salt and freshly ground black pepper*

PREPARATION

1 Trim off any beetroot leaves, leaving at least
10cm (4in) of stem still attached to prevent the
colour of the beetroot bleeding as it cooks. Place
in a saucepan, cover with cold water and bring to
the boil. Reduce the heat, cover and cook until the
beetroot are tender when pierced with the point
of a knife: at least 1 hour.
2 Allow to cool, then peel off the skin using your
fingers and a sharp knife and cut the beetroot into
julienne strips (see page 145). Place in a saucepan
to reheat when you want to eat it.

 *You can prepare the beetroot several hours
ahead to this point.*

3 Remove the pith from the orange peel and cut
the peel into long thin strips. Add the peel and
juice to the beetroot, along with the butter, and
season to taste. Cover, heat through and serve.

GREEN BEANS WITH CUMIN

*I love green beans and find they go with many dishes.
When very young and tender, they can be steam-boiled
whole and need no embellishment. When they are
bigger, trim them, and jazz them up with some
spicy cumin seeds. Serves 4.*

INGREDIENTS

*750g (1½lb) green beans, trimmed
15g (½oz) butter
15ml (1 tbsp) olive oil
2 tsps cumin seeds
salt and freshly ground black pepper*

PREPARATION

1 Pour 1cm (½in) of boiling water into a saucepan
and add the green beans. Cover the pan and half-
boil, half-steam the beans over a moderate heat
until just tender but still crisp: 2–5 minutes
depending on size. Drain and transfer to a bowl.
2 Melt the butter with the oil in a frying pan over
a moderate heat. Add the cumin seeds and stir
until they begin to pop and smell aromatic:
1–2 minutes. Pour the seeds along with the
butter and oil over the beans. Toss the beans
lightly, season to taste and serve at once.

BUTTERED LEEKS WITH PARSLEY

*Tender, not-too-large leeks are best for this, but in any
case try to get leeks that are of similar diameter so they
cook in the same amount of time. Serves 4.*

INGREDIENTS

*1kg (2lb) thin leeks
15–30g (½–1oz) butter
2 tbsps finely chopped flat-leaf parsley
freshly grated nutmeg
salt and freshly ground black pepper*

PREPARATION

1 Trim the leeks and wash them of dirt as shown
on page 147.
2 Pour 1cm (½in) of boiling water into a large
saucepan or frying pan and lay the leeks in it.
Cover and half-boil, half-steam until tender:
7–10 minutes depending on size. Drain. Transfer
to a bowl that can accommodate them lengthways.
3 Add the butter, parsley and freshly grated
nutmeg. Season with salt and black pepper, toss
the leeks well and serve at once.

CELERIAC PUREE

*One of the nicest ways to serve the root vegetable celeriac
is as a creamy purée, with plenty of salt and freshly
ground black pepper. Sometimes I use celeriac on its own,
but I find a mixture of potato and celeriac works
particularly well because the potatoes add a starchy
creaminess to the mixture. Serves 4.*

INGREDIENTS

*500g (1lb) celeriac
250g (8oz) potatoes
15g (½oz) butter
a little milk or single cream
salt and freshly ground black pepper*

PREPARATION

1 Peel the celeriac and the potatoes. I find a sharp
knife is best for the celeriac and a swivel-bladed
peeler for the potatoes. Cut into even-sized
chunks, place in a saucepan and cover with boiling
water. Put the lid on the pan and simmer the
vegetables gently until tender: 15–20 minutes.
2 Drain, saving the water for stock. Add the
butter and mash with a potato masher (don't use a
food processor because this makes the potatoes
glue-like), softening the mixture with milk or
cream. Season to taste. Serve at once or keep
warm for up to an hour in a bain-marie on the hob.

SPINACH WITH NUTMEG

*If you can get tender spinach leaves, wilting them in a
little olive oil is more successful than boiling them:
it retains their bright green colour and fresh taste. You
need a large saucepan for this; it may be easier
to cook in two batches. Serves 4.*

INGREDIENTS

*750g (1½lb) tender young spinach leaves
30ml (2 tbsps) olive oil
freshly grated nutmeg
salt and freshly ground black pepper*

PREPARATION

1 Wash the spinach thoroughly in 2 or 3 changes
of cold water, then put it into a colander to drain.
2 Heat a tablespoonful of oil in a large saucepan
over a high heat. Add half the spinach and stir-fry
until it has just wilted and warmed through:
1–2 minutes. Remove from the heat and transfer
to a warmed bowl. Cook the second batch of
spinach in the same way, using the remaining oil.
3 Stir in the nutmeg, salt and pepper, and serve.

*Carrot and courgette
ribbons with pesto
(page 82)*

*Bombay potatoes
(page 86)*

*Spiced red cabbage
and apple (page 87)*

SPICED OKRA

*Okra is a vegetable you either love or hate. I love it;
I find that its fresh flavour and glutinous texture
lend themselves especially well to spicy mixtures
such as this. Serves 4.*

INGREDIENTS

*30ml (2 tbsps) groundnut or sunflower oil
1 medium-sized onion, chopped
2 cloves garlic, chopped
2 tsps ground cumin
2 tsps ground coriander
500g (1lb) okra, stalk ends removed,
cut into 6mm (¼in) lengths
400g (14oz) can whole tomatoes, coarsely
chopped, with juice
salt and freshly ground black pepper
2–4 tbsps chopped fresh coriander, to serve*

PREPARATION

1 Warm the oil in a medium-sized saucepan
over a moderate heat, add the onion, cover and
cook for 5 minutes.
2 Add the garlic, cumin and coriander and cook
for 2 minutes, stirring from time to time.
3 Add the okra and cook for a further 2 minutes,
stirring from time to time.
4 Pour in the tomatoes with their juice and cook,
uncovered, until the okra is tender and the excess
tomato liquid has evaporated to make a thick
sauce: 15–20 minutes.
5 Season with salt and black pepper to taste and
serve, sprinkled with chopped coriander.

BOMBAY POTATOES

*These golden potatoes can be served as a side dish
with a curry or a pilau, or with any bean or grain
dish when you want to add a little spiciness.
Illustrated on pages 84–5. Serves 4.*

INGREDIENTS

*30ml (2 tbsps) groundnut or sunflower oil
1 medium-sized onion, chopped
2 cloves garlic, chopped
2 tsps ground cumin
2 tsps ground coriander
½ tsp turmeric
¼tsp cayenne pepper
750g (1½lb) potatoes, peeled and
cut into 1cm (½in) dice
salt
1 tsp garam masala
freshly ground black pepper
2–4 tbsps chopped fresh coriander, to serve*

PREPARATION

1 Warm the oil in a medium-sized saucepan
over a moderate heat, add the onion, cover and
cook for 5 minutes.
2 Add the garlic, cumin, ground coriander,
turmeric and cayenne and cook for 2 minutes,
stirring from time to time.
3 Add the potatoes and stir well to coat them
with the onion, garlic and spices. Add a teaspoon
of salt and pour in 150ml (5fl oz) water, bring to
the boil, then cover and cook over a gentle heat
until the potato is just tender and most of the
water has disappeared: about 10–15 minutes.
4 Stir in the garam masala. Taste the mixture. If
you like, add more salt, some black pepper and, if
you want a hotter dish, some more cayenne. Serve
warm or cool, sprinkled with chopped coriander.

SPICED RED CABBAGE & APPLE

This aromatic vegetable dish is just as good, if not better, when reheated. It is a warming dish to make as part of a winter meal and is the perfect accompaniment for a baked potato filled with soured cream and chives. Illustrated on page 85. Serves 4.

INGREDIENTS

30g (1oz) butter
15ml (1 tbsp) groundnut or sunflower oil
1 large onion, chopped
350g (12oz) cooking or dessert apples, peeled, cored and chopped
750g (1½lb) red cabbage, core removed, leaves shredded
pinch of ground cloves
½ tsp ground cinnamon
60g (2oz) sultanas or raisins, optional
1 tbsp brown sugar
15ml (1 tbsp) red wine vinegar
salt and freshly ground black pepper

PREPARATION

1 Melt the butter with the oil in a large saucepan over a moderate heat, add the onion, cover and cook for 5 minutes.
2 Add the apples, stir, cover and cook for a further 2 – 3 minutes.
3 Add the cabbage to the pan and pour in 450ml (15fl oz) water. Stir in the cloves, cinnamon, sultanas or raisins, sugar and vinegar. Reduce the heat, cover and cook until the cabbage is very tender: about 1 hour.
4 Season well with salt and black pepper and serve at once or reheat later.

GRILLED POTATOES WITH GARLIC & ROSEMARY

This is a good way to prepare potatoes towards the end of summer when they are larger. I generally leave the skins on the boiled potatoes, but they slip off easily with a knife. Serves 4.

INGREDIENTS

750g – 1kg (1½ – 2lb) potatoes, scrubbed
olive oil, to brush over the potatoes
4 cloves garlic, peeled
3 – 4 sprigs of rosemary
sea salt and freshly ground black pepper

PREPARATION

1 Cut the potatoes into even-sized pieces for cooking. Put in a saucepan, cover with water and boil until they are almost tender when pierced with the point of a knife. Drain and allow to cool. Slip off the skins if desired. Cut the potatoes into slices about 6mm (¼in) thick.
2 Preheat the grill to high.
3 Place the potatoes in a single layer on an oiled baking sheet or in the grill pan and brush with olive oil. Grill until they are crisp and golden brown on one side, then turn them over and crisp the other side.
4 Roughly chop the garlic and rosemary. Sprinkle these over the potatoes a few minutes before they are done; if you add them too soon they will burn and spoil the flavour.
5 Sprinkle with sea salt, grind some black pepper over them and serve at once.

PASTA

Pasta is popular with just about everyone: quick to cook, and the basis for many exciting and delicious meals. A dish of pasta with one of the tempting sauces on these pages creates a complete meal that can be made in minutes; or serve as starters for a larger party. With a little more time, you can put together a wonderful baked pasta dish, spinach, tomato and mozzarella lasagne, that is perfect for entertaining. Prepare it ahead of time and relax.

LINGUINE WITH CREAM & HERB SAUCE

Serves 4.

INGREDIENTS

15g (½ oz) butter
1 shallot or small onion, chopped
400g (14oz) low-fat crème fraîche
salt and freshly ground black pepper
500g (1lb) linguine
15ml (1 tbsp) olive oil
2 – 4 tbsps chopped fresh herbs such as parsley, chives and chervil
freshly grated Parmesan cheese, optional

PREPARATION

1 Pour 4 litres (7 pints) of water into a large pan and place over a high heat. This is for the pasta.
2 Melt the butter in a medium-sized saucepan over a moderate heat, add the shallot or onion, cover and cook until tender: about 4 minutes.
3 Add the crème fraîche, heat to boiling point and cook, stirring, until thick and creamy: 2 – 3 minutes. Season with salt and black pepper and keep warm.
4 When the water reaches a rolling boil, drop in the pasta. Bring back to the boil, give the pasta a quick stir, then let the water boil steadily until the pasta is *al dente*: tender but not soft right through. Bite a piece to check.
5 Drain the pasta but leave some water clinging to it, and return it to the hot pan with the olive oil and a good seasoning of salt and black pepper. Toss the pasta so that it is coated with the oil.
6 Add the sauce to the pasta, together with the fresh herbs. Toss the pasta, making sure that it is well coated with the sauce, and serve at once, with freshly grated Parmesan if liked.

FARFALLE WITH BROCCOLI CREAM SAUCE

Serves 4.

INGREDIENTS

15g (½ oz) butter
1 shallot or small onion, chopped
400g (14oz) low-fat crème fraîche
salt and freshly ground black pepper
125g (4oz) broccoli florets
500g (1lb) farfalle, or other chunky pasta
15ml (1 tbsp) olive oil
freshly grated Parmesan cheese, optional

PREPARATION

1 Pour 4 litres (7 pints) of water into a large pan and place over a high heat. This is for the pasta.
2 Melt the butter in a medium-sized saucepan over a moderate heat, add the shallot or onion, cover and cook until tender: about 4 minutes.
3 Add the crème fraîche, heat to boiling point and cook, stirring, until thick and creamy: 2 – 3 minutes. Season with salt and black pepper and keep warm.
4 Put the broccoli in a small pan, cover with boiling water and cook until just tender: 2 – 3 minutes. Drain well, and stir into the sauce.
5 To cook and serve the pasta, follow steps 4 to 6 of Linguine with cream and herb sauce, omitting the fresh herbs in step 6.

TAGLIATELLE WITH MUSHROOM CREAM SAUCE

Serves 4.

INGREDIENTS

*15g (½ oz) butter
1 shallot or small onion, chopped
125g (4oz) button mushrooms, sliced
400g (14oz) low-fat crème fraîche
salt and freshly ground black pepper
500g (1lb) tagliatelle
15ml (1 tbsp) olive oil
freshly grated Parmesan cheese, optional*

PREPARATION

1 Pour 4 litres (7 pints) of water into a large pan and place over a high heat. This is for the pasta.
2 Melt the butter in a medium-sized saucepan over a moderate heat, add the shallot or onion, cover and cook for 2 minutes. Add the mushrooms and cook until tender: around 2 more minutes.
3 Add the crème fraîche, heat to boiling point and cook, stirring, until thick and creamy: 2 3 minutes. Season with salt and black pepper and keep warm.
4 To cook and serve the pasta, follow steps 4 to 6 of Linguine with cream and herb sauce (page 88), omitting the fresh herbs in step 6.

SPAGHETTI WITH BLUE CHEESE SAUCE

Serves 4.

INGREDIENTS

*15g (½ oz) butter
1 shallot or small onion, chopped
400g (14oz) low-fat crème fraîche
salt and freshly ground black pepper
500g (1lb) spaghetti
15ml (1 tbsp) olive oil
60 – 125g (2 – 4oz) Dolcelatte or
Gorgonzola cheese, crumbled
freshly grated Parmesan cheese, optional*

PREPARATION

1 Follow steps 1 to 5 of Linguine with cream and herb sauce (page 88).
2 Add the sauce to the pasta, together with the blue cheese. Toss the pasta, making sure that it is well coated with the sauce, and serve at once, with freshly grated Parmesan if liked.

SPINACH, TOMATO & MOZZARELLA LASAGNE

Rich-tasting lasagne in abundance, with plenty of leafy salad and good bread, makes an excellent spread for a party, whatever the age group. Lasagne is quite fiddly to prepare but it is based on two simple sauces, tomato and béchamel, that can be made ahead of time. Indeed, the whole lasagne can be assembled in advance and kept in a cool place or the refrigerator until you want to bake it for ravenous guests. Serves 4.

INGREDIENTS

*15g (½oz) butter
200g (7oz) frozen spinach or fresh tender spinach leaves
salt and freshly ground black pepper
250g (8oz) lasagne
1 quantity of basic tomato sauce (page 121),
prepared ahead
150g (5oz) mozzarella cheese, thinly sliced
150ml (5fl oz) single cream
1 quantity of béchamel sauce (page 148),
prepared ahead
30 – 60g (1 – 2oz) freshly grated Parmesan cheese*

PREPARATION

1 Preheat the oven to 180°C / 350°F / gas 4, unless preparing the lasagne ahead to bake later.
2 Melt the butter in a large saucepan over a moderate heat, add the spinach and cook until tender: 7 minutes for fresh spinach, 2 – 3 minutes for frozen. Drain well, press out excess water and season with salt and black pepper.
3 Parboil the pasta: pour 4 litres (7 pints) of water into a large saucepan and bring to the boil. Drop several sheets of the pasta into the boiling water and cook for a few seconds. Retrieve the sheets with a slotted spoon, drape them over the sides of a colander to prevent them sticking together, and do the next batch. Repeat until all the pasta is done.
4 Grease an ovenproof dish or baking tin, about 24 x 32 cm (9½ x 13in) and 7.5cm (3in) deep. Cover the base with lasagne and build up the layers as follows: half the tomato sauce, all the spinach, another layer of lasagne, the rest of the tomato sauce, all the mozzarella, the rest of the lasagne.
5 Stir the cream into the béchamel sauce and pour evenly over the lasagne. Sprinkle Parmesan on top.

You can prepare ahead to this point. Keep the assembled lasagne in a cool place or the refrigerator until you are ready to bake it.

6 Bake the lasagne until bubbling and golden brown on top: 40 – 50 minutes. Serve at once.

SPAGHETTI WITH FRESH TOMATO SAUCE

Though this is one of the simplest pasta sauce recipes, the combination of perfectly cooked pasta and fresh tomato sauce is hard to beat. Once familiar with the basic recipe, you can vary it by adding other ingredients and flavourings of your choice. Two cans of tomatoes in juice can be used instead of the fresh tomatoes: cook uncovered until most of the liquid has evaporated, to leave you with a thick sauce. Serves 4.

INGREDIENTS

45 ml (3 tbsps) olive oil
1 large onion, chopped
2 cloves garlic, chopped
1 kg (2 lb) fresh tomatoes, peeled and chopped
salt and freshly ground black pepper
500 g (1 lb) spaghetti
fresh Parmesan cheese, cut into flakes, optional
fresh basil leaves, to garnish

PREPARATION

1 Pour 4 litres (7 pints) of water into a large pan for the pasta and place over a high heat.
2 Warm 30 ml (2 tbsps) of the olive oil in a saucepan over a moderate heat, add the onion, cover and cook until tender: about 5 minutes. Add the garlic and cook for a further 2 minutes.
3 Reduce the heat, add the tomatoes, cover and cook until they have collapsed and the sauce has thickened: 10–15 minutes. Season to taste with salt and black pepper and keep warm.
4 Meanwhile, when the water reaches a rolling boil, drop in the pasta. Bring back to the boil, give the pasta a quick stir, then let the water boil steadily until the pasta is *al dente*: tender but not soft right through. Bite a piece to check.
5 Drain the pasta but leave some water clinging to it, and return it to the hot pan with the remaining tablespoon of olive oil and a good seasoning of salt and black pepper. Toss the pasta to coat it with oil.
6 Add the sauce to the pasta and toss it well, making sure that the pasta is well coated with the sauce. Serve at once, with flakes of Parmesan if liked, and basil leaves to garnish.

PENNE ARRABBIATA

This is a tomato sauce with chilli added to give it a kick. Like the previous recipe, it is very easy to make — the whole dish can be made from start to finish in about 20 minutes. Serves 4.

INGREDIENTS

45 ml (3 tbsps) olive oil
1 large onion, chopped
2 cloves garlic, chopped
1 fresh green chilli, deseeded and finely chopped
2 x 400 g (14 oz) cans whole peeled tomatoes, coarsely chopped, with juice
salt and freshly ground black pepper
500 g (1 lb) penne, or other tubular pasta such as rigatoni
fresh Parmesan cheese, cut into flakes, optional
fresh basil leaves, to garnish

PREPARATION

1 Pour 4 litres (7 pints) of water into a large pan and place over a high heat. This is for the pasta.
2 Warm 30 ml (2 tbsps) of the olive oil in a saucepan over a moderate heat, add the onion, cover and cook until tender: about 5 minutes. Add the garlic and chilli and cook for a further 2 minutes.
3 Pour in the tomatoes with their juice and cook, uncovered, until the excess tomato liquid has evaporated and the sauce has reduced: 10–15 minutes. Season to taste with salt and black pepper and keep warm.
4 Meanwhile, when the water reaches a rolling boil, drop in the pasta. Bring back to the boil, give the pasta a quick stir, then let the water boil steadily until the pasta is *al dente*: tender but not soft right through. Bite a piece to check.
5 Drain the pasta but leave some water clinging to it, and return it to the hot pan with the remaining tablespoon of olive oil and a good seasoning of salt and black pepper. Toss the pasta to coat it with oil.
6 Add the sauce to the pasta and toss it well, making sure that the pasta is well coated with the sauce. Serve at once, with flakes of Parmesan if liked, and basil leaves to garnish.

RIGATONI WITH TOMATO, AUBERGINE & RED PEPPERS

This sauce goes well with a tubular pasta such as rigatoni or a long pasta such as spaghetti. It benefits from slower cooking than the tomato sauces on the facing page, becoming a rich sauce that is delicious accompanied by a leafy green salad and a glass of red wine. Serves 4.

INGREDIENTS

*45ml (3 tbsps) olive oil
1 large onion, chopped
1 medium-sized aubergine, cut into fine dice
1 red pepper, cored, deseeded and cut into fine dice
1 clove garlic, chopped
2 x 400g (14oz) cans whole peeled tomatoes, coarsely chopped, with juice
salt and freshly ground black pepper
500g (1lb) rigatoni
fresh Parmesan cheese, cut into flakes, optional
fresh basil leaves, to garnish*

PREPARATION

1 Warm 30ml (2 tbsps) of the olive oil in a saucepan over a moderate heat, add the onion, cover and cook until tender: about 5 minutes. Add the aubergine, pepper and garlic, cover and cook for a further 5 minutes, stirring occasionally.
2 Pour in the tomatoes with their juice, reduce the heat and cook slowly, uncovered, until the excess liquid has evaporated and the sauce is thick and purée-like: 20–25 minutes. Season to taste with salt and black pepper and keep warm.
3 Pour 4 litres (7 pints) of water into a large pan over a high heat and bring to the boil. Drop in the pasta, give it a quick stir, then let the water boil steadily until the pasta is *al dente*: tender but not soft right through. Bite a piece to check.
4 Drain the pasta but leave some water clinging to it, and return it to the hot pan with the remaining tablespoon of olive oil and a good seasoning of salt and pepper. Toss the pasta to coat it with the oil.
5 Pour in the sauce and toss the pasta once more. Serve at once, with flakes of Parmesan if liked, and basil leaves to garnish.

EGGS & CHEESE

Delicious and versatile foods in their own right, eggs and cheese are invaluable ingredients in many tempting dishes, from the lightest of soufflés to vibrant, savoury roulades and simple omelettes. To offset their richness, serve these dishes with lightly cooked vegetables and a fresh fruit dessert.

CHEESE FONDUE

A delicious, runny cheese fondue is usually a winner. It is too rich to eat every day, but it is perfect for a small party, when spearing cubes of bread on to a fork and dipping them into the fondue is all part of the fun, and so, too, is scraping out the delicious crusty cheese mixture from the bottom of the pan. You need a burner to stand the saucepan of cheese on: a fondue burner or a nightlight plate-warmer will do. Serves 4.

INGREDIENTS

1 clove garlic, peeled and halved
300ml (½ pint) dry white wine or cider
250g (8oz) Gruyère cheese, grated
250g (8oz) Emmental cheese, grated
1 tsp potato flour or cornflour
30ml (2 tbsps) kirsch
freshly grated nutmeg
salt and freshly ground black pepper
1 large baguette, cut into bite-sized pieces and
warmed in the oven, to serve

PREPARATION

1 Rub the garlic around the inside of a medium-sized saucepan, then discard it. Put the wine or cider and cheeses into the saucepan and heat gently, stirring often with a wooden spoon, until the cheese has melted and the mixture comes just to the boil. Remove from the heat.
2 Mix the potato flour or cornflour with the kirsch and stir into the cheese mixture. Return to the heat and stir until the fondue thickens and coats the back of the spoon. Season with nutmeg, salt and black pepper.
3 Place the pan of fondue in the centre of the table on a burner and serve with the warmed bread cubes. Forks are best for spearing the cubes of bread and dipping them into the fondue. The fondue becomes thicker the longer it stands on the burner, and it leaves a lovely cheesy residue in the bottom of the pan that should be eaten too.

SPINACH SOUFFLE

A basic soufflé mixture can be flavoured with a variety of different ingredients, and one of the best is spinach. For an even more flavoursome soufflé, add the Parmesan cheese. Serves 3 to 4.

INGREDIENTS

60g (2oz) butter, plus extra to grease the dish
400g (14oz) frozen chopped spinach or
fresh young spinach leaves
45g (1½oz) plain flour
300ml (½ pint) milk
5 free-range eggs, separated (with 1 yolk unused)
45g (1½oz) freshly grated Parmesan cheese, optional
freshly grated nutmeg
salt and freshly ground black pepper

PREPARATION

1 Melt 15g (½oz) of the butter in a large saucepan over a moderate heat and add the spinach. For frozen spinach, cook until it has thawed and any water has evaporated: 2–3 minutes. For fresh, cook until tender: about 7 minutes. Drain, squeezing out excess water, and chop.
2 Melt the rest of the butter, stir in the flour, and slowly add the milk to make a béchamel sauce, as shown on page 148. Leave to cool slightly.
3 Stir four of the egg yolks into the sauce (save the fifth yolk to use in another recipe). Add the spinach and, if used, the Parmesan. Season with nutmeg, salt and pepper.

You can prepare ahead up to this point. The spinach mixture and the egg whites keep for several hours, covered, in the refrigerator.

4 Preheat the oven to 200°C/400°F/gas 6. Butter a 1.5-litre (2½-pint) soufflé dish and tie a piece of buttered nonstick paper around the outside extending at least 5cm (2in) above the rim.
5 To finish making the soufflé and to bake it, follow steps 4–6 on page 26 of Classic Dishes.

TWICE-BAKED GOAT'S CHEESE & THYME SOUFFLES

The easiest soufflés are these small, twice-baked ones: bake them once, then put them aside. Later, turn them out of their containers on to a baking sheet and return to a hot oven until golden and puffed up. Serves 6 as a first course, 3 as a main course.

INGREDIENTS

60g (2oz) butter
45g (1½oz) flour
300ml (½ pint) milk
5 free-range eggs, separated (with 1 yolk unused)
125g (4oz) firm goat's cheese (preferably with rind), cut into 6mm (¼in) dice
salt and freshly ground black pepper
butter and dry grated Parmesan to coat the ramekins
300ml (½ pint) single cream, optional
60g (2oz) soft fresh breadcrumbs
2 tbsps chopped fresh thyme

PREPARATION

1 Melt the butter, stir in the flour, and slowly add the milk to make a béchamel sauce, as shown on page 148. Leave to cool slightly.
2 Stir four of the egg yolks into the sauce (save the fifth yolk to use in another recipe). Add the goat's cheese and season with salt and black pepper.
3 Preheat the oven to 200°C/400°F/gas 6. Butter 6 x 180ml (6fl oz) ramekins or tins and sprinkle with dry grated Parmesan.
4 In a greasefree bowl, whisk the five egg whites until they are stiff but not so dry that you can slice them. Stir 2 tablespoons of egg white into the cheese mixture, then gently fold in the rest using a metal spoon. Pour the mixture into the ramekins.
5 Put the ramekins into a bain-marie (see page 147) and place in the oven. Turn the temperature down to 190°C/375°F/gas 5. Bake the soufflés until risen and a skewer comes out clean: 15–20 minutes. Remove from the oven and leave to cool in their containers; they will sink a great deal.

 You can prepare ahead up to this point. Keep the soufflés in their containers in the refrigerator for 2–3 days or in the freezer for several weeks.

6 Preheat the oven to 220°C/425°F/gas 7. Turn out the soufflés – into your hand is easiest – then place in a shallow ovenproof dish.
7 Pour the cream, if liked, over and around the soufflés. Mix the breadcrumbs and thyme, and sprinkle generously over the top. Bake until risen, heated through and golden brown: about 15 minutes. Serve at once from the baking dish.

TWICE-BAKED MUSHROOM SOUFFLES

Serves 6 as a first course, 3 as a main course.

INGREDIENTS

60g (2oz) butter
125g (4oz) button mushrooms, chopped
45g (1½oz) flour
300ml (½ pint) milk
5 free-range eggs, separated (with 1 yolk unused)
3 tbsps chopped mixed fresh herbs, such as parsley, marjoram, chives and thyme
60g (2oz) Gruyère cheese, grated
salt and freshly ground black pepper
butter and dry grated Parmesan to coat the ramekins
300ml (½ pint) single cream, optional
30g (1oz) freshly grated Parmesan cheese, optional

PREPARATION

1 Melt the butter in a medium-sized saucepan over a moderate heat, add the mushrooms and cook, uncovered, for 2–3 minutes.
2 Stir in the flour and slowly add the milk to make a béchamel sauce, as shown on page 148. Leave to cool slightly.
3 Stir four of the egg yolks into the sauce (save the fifth to use in another recipe). Add the herbs, half the Gruyère and season with salt and pepper.
4 Preheat the oven to 200°C/400°F/gas 6. Butter 6 x 180ml (6fl oz) ramekins or tins and sprinkle with dry grated Parmesan.
5 In a greasefree bowl, whisk the five egg whites until they are stiff but not so dry that you can slice them. Stir 2 tablespoons of egg white into the mushroom mixture, then fold in the rest using a metal spoon. Pour the mixture into the ramekins.
6 Put the ramekins into a bain-marie (see page 147) and place in the oven. Turn the temperature down to 190°C/375°F/gas 5. Bake the soufflés until risen and a skewer comes out clean: 15–20 minutes. Remove from the oven and leave to cool in their containers; they will sink a great deal.

 You can prepare ahead up to this point. Keep the soufflés in their containers in the refrigerator for 2–3 days or in the freezer for several weeks.

7 Preheat the oven to 220°C/425°F/gas 7. Turn out the soufflés – into your hand is easiest – then place in a shallow ovenproof dish.
8 Pour the cream, if liked, over and around the soufflés, sprinkle with the rest of the Gruyère and, if desired, the Parmesan. Bake until risen, heated through and golden brown: about 15 minutes. Serve at once from the baking dish.

CHEESE ROULADE BASE

The roulades on the right are made with this cheese base. They are illustrated on pages 36–7. Each serves 6 as a starter, 4 as a main course.

INGREDIENTS

butter and dry grated Parmesan for coating
60g (2oz) curd cheese
150ml (5fl oz) single cream
4 free-range eggs, separated
200g (7oz) hard cheese, such as Gruyère or Cheddar, grated
3 tbsps chopped fresh herbs, such as thyme, marjoram and parsley, optional
salt and freshly ground black pepper
freshly grated Parmesan cheese to garnish, optional

PREPARATION

1 Preheat the oven to 200°C/400°F/gas 6. Line a 22 x 32cm (9 x 13in) Swiss-roll tin with nonstick paper. Grease the paper lightly with butter and sprinkle with dry Parmesan cheese.
2 Put the curd cheese into a large bowl, add the cream and mix until smooth. Beat in the egg yolks one by one. Finally, stir in the grated cheese, and the herbs if desired, and season to taste.
3 In a separate greasefree bowl, whisk the egg whites until they are stiff but not so dry that you can slice them. Fold the egg whites into the cheese mixture using a metal spoon, then pour the cheese and egg white mixture into the prepared tin, smoothing it to the edges. Bake until risen and just firm in the centre: 12–15 minutes.
4 Place a piece of nonstick paper, large enough for the roulade, next to the oven and sprinkle it with Parmesan. Take the roulade out of the oven and turn it out, face down, on to the paper. Peel the nonstick paper that was used to line the tin from the top of the roulade.
5 Allow the roulade to become cool to the touch before covering with the chosen filling and rolling up as shown opposite. Sprinkle the finished roulade with freshly grated Parmesan if desired. It may be served at once or reheated later. Some roulades, such as Gruyère and herb with rocket (right), benefit from being cooled in the refrigerator before serving.

 Roulades may be prepared in advance and reheated. Wrap in foil and place in a preheated oven (160°C/325°F/gas 3) for 15 minutes.

—— *Roulade fillings* ——

GRUYERE WITH RED PEPPERS

INGREDIENTS

4 large red peppers, quartered
125g (4oz) curd cheese
cheese roulade base, using Gruyère and omitting herbs

PREPARATION

1 Grill and peel the peppers as shown on page 144 and remove the stalk and seeds.
2 Soften the curd cheese with about 30ml (2 tbsps) of water. Spread it over the roulade base, cover with the peppers and roll up as shown. Serve with quick herb sauce (page 123).

CHEDDAR & HERB WITH MUSHROOMS

INGREDIENTS

30g (1oz) butter
600g (1¼lb) mushrooms, thinly sliced
2 cloves garlic, finely chopped
salt and freshly ground black pepper
cheese roulade base, using Cheddar and herbs

PREPARATION

1 Melt the butter in a saucepan over a moderate heat, add the mushrooms and garlic and cook until the mushrooms are tender and the liquid has evaporated: 12–15 minutes. Season to taste.
2 Cover the base with the mushrooms and roll up as shown. Serve with red wine sauce (page 121).

GRUYERE & HERBS WITH ROCKET

INGREDIENTS

cheese roulade base, using Gruyère and herbs
2 ripe avocado pears
30ml (2 tbsps) lemon juice
30g (1oz) rocket, shredded

PREPARATION

1 Cover the roulade base with a damp tea towel and set aside to cool; this roulade is eaten cold.
2 Mash the flesh of the avocados with the lemon juice and spread over the cooled roulade base.
3 Scatter the rocket over the roulade and roll up as shown. Chill in the refrigerator for one hour before serving with fresh tomato sauce (page 121).

ROLLING UP A GRUYERE WITH RED PEPPER ROULADE

1 Spread the curd cheese over the roulade base, leaving a border of about 1cm (½in) all round to make the roulade easier to roll.

2 Cover with red peppers, then roll up the roulade, starting from a short side (this gives a thick roulade). Use the paper to help lift the base as you roll it.

3 Place the roulade with the seam underneath so it cannot unroll. Trim the ends and, if liked, sprinkle the top with freshly grated Parmesan.

Gruyère with red pepper roulade, served with quick herb sauce

CASHEW NUT ROULADE WITH BROCCOLI

This very rich roulade, shown on page 37, is ideal as the centrepiece for a special dinner. Serves 6 as a starter, 4 as a main course.

INGREDIENTS

4 free-range eggs
salt and freshly ground black pepper
200g (7oz) roasted, unsalted cashew nuts
2 cloves garlic
THE FILLING
1 quantity hollandaise sauce (page 123)
500g (1lb) broccoli, trimmed and cut into small pieces
salt and freshly ground black pepper

PREPARATION

1 Preheat the oven to 200°C/400°F/gas 6. Line a 22 x 32cm (9 x 13in) Swiss-roll tin with nonstick paper to extend slightly up the sides.
2 Break the eggs into a large bowl, add salt and black pepper and beat until the mixture is thick and the trail left by the beaters is visible. This is done quickly using an electric whisk; with a hand whisk it takes 5–10 minutes.
3 Put the cashew nuts and garlic into a food processor or blender and work until they are chopped finely but not oily and pulverized.
4 Stir two-thirds of the chopped nuts and garlic into the eggs and then pour this mixture into the prepared tin, smoothing it to the edges. Bake until just firm and spongy in the centre: 6–8 minutes.
5 Place a piece of nonstick paper, large enough for the roulade, next to the oven and sprinkle it with the remaining chopped nuts and garlic. Remove the roulade from the oven and turn it out, face down, on to the paper. Peel the nonstick paper that was used to line the tin from the top.
6 Prepare the hollandaise as described on page 123.
7 Put the broccoli in a pan, pour in a little boiling water, cover and half-boil, half-steam until just tender and still bright green: 3 minutes. Drain.
8 Lightly spread the roulade base with some of the hollandaise sauce, then cover with an even layer of the broccoli. Roll up the roulade from one of the short sides (as shown on page 95).
9 Serve at once with the remaining hollandaise.

SPINACH ROULADE WITH CREAM CHEESE & PEPPERS

Illustrated on page 36, this roulade can be made in advance and reheated as described on page 94. Serves 6 as a starter, 4 as a main course.

INGREDIENTS

500g (1lb) fresh young spinach leaves
15g (½oz) butter
4 free-range eggs, separated
freshly grated nutmeg
salt and freshly ground black pepper
4 tbsps dry grated Parmesan for coating
THE FILLING
1 large red pepper, quartered
250g (8oz) cream cheese
a little milk

PREPARATION

1 Preheat the oven to 200°C/400°F/gas 6. Line a 22 x 32cm (9 x 13in) Swiss-roll tin with nonstick paper to extend slightly up the sides.
2 Place the spinach in a pan with just the water that clings to its leaves after washing. Cook over a moderate heat until tender: 7–10 minutes. Drain.
3 Put the spinach, butter and egg yolks in a blender, and work until smooth. Transfer to a large bowl and season with nutmeg, salt and pepper.
4 In a separate bowl, whisk the egg whites until they are stiff but not so dry that you can slice them. Fold the egg whites into the spinach mixture using a metal spoon, then pour the spinach and egg white mixture into the prepared tin, smoothing it to the edges.
5 Sprinkle 2 tablespoons of the Parmesan cheese over the roulade. Bake the roulade until just firm and spongy in the centre: 12–15 minutes.
6 Place a piece of nonstick paper, large enough for the roulade, next to the oven and sprinkle it with the remaining Parmesan. Remove the roulade from the oven and turn it out, face down, on to the paper. Peel the nonstick paper that was used to line the tin from the top.
7 Grill and peel the pepper as shown on page 144, remove the stalk and seeds, and cut into strips.
8 Beat the cream cheese with enough milk to make it spreadable, then cover the roulade with it. Arrange the red pepper over the top in widely spaced stripes, then roll up the roulade from one of the short sides (as shown on page 95).
9 Serve with yellow pepper sauce (page 120).

DEEP-FRIED BRIE WITH APRICOT SAUCE

Gooey Brie in a crisp coating of crumbs is delicious, particularly if it is accompanied by a sweet sauce such as apricot, or served with sweet mango chutney. Deep-fried Brie is most often served as a first course but I prefer it as a main course with steamed vegetables or a leafy salad to balance its richness. It needs to be eaten immediately so is best made for only a small number of people unless you have a very large deep-frier. Serves 3 as a starter, 2 as a main course.

INGREDIENTS

250g (8oz) Brie
1 free-range egg, beaten
2 tbsps plain flour, to coat
10 tbsps breadcrumbs, to coat
groundnut oil for deep-frying
APRICOT SAUCE
125g (4oz) apricot jam
lemon juice, to taste

PREPARATION

1 Cut the Brie into six even-sized portions. Dip the pieces of Brie first in the egg, then in the flour, then in the egg again and finally in the breadcrumbs, coating the pieces well so the cheese cannot ooze out during frying.
2 For the sauce, put the jam into a small saucepan with 30ml (2 tbsps) of water, place over a low heat and stir until the jam has melted. Add a squeeze or two of lemon juice to taste.
3 Fill a deep saucepan or deep-frier no more than half-full with oil and place over a high heat. Once the oil reaches 180°C/350°F – when bubbles form on the handle of a wooden spoon stirred into the oil – it is ready for deep-frying.
4 Using a slotted spoon, place the portions of Brie in the hot oil (you may need to do two batches). The cheese should rise to the surface and start browning at once. As soon as the pieces are golden brown all over, remove with the slotted spoon and place on a plate lined with crumpled kitchen paper. Quickly reheat the oil and put in the second batch, if necessary. Serve at once, with the sauce.

DEEP-FRIED CREPE PARCELS WITH GOAT'S CHEESE FILLING

These are not as fiddly to make as they might sound and the result is fabulous: a crisp coating of crumbs on a light crêpe enclosing a filling of melting goat's cheese. I particularly enjoy the sharpness of goat's cheese, but other cheeses can be used: Brie or Camembert, for example, or even blue cheese. I like something sweet with them, such as cranberry sauce, especially if it is around Christmas time. Serves 4.

INGREDIENTS

½ quantity of crêpe batter (page 149)
olive oil for cooking the crêpes
THE FILLING
250g (8oz) firm goat's cheese (the type often sold in a log), cut into thin slices or small dice, including the rind
THE COATING
2 free-range eggs, beaten
125g (4oz) fresh or dried breadcrumbs, to coat
groundnut oil for deep-frying

PREPARATION

1 Use the batter to make 4 large thin crêpes, about 20cm (8in) in diameter.
2 Divide the goat's cheese among the four crêpes, placing it in the centre of each one. Fold the sides into the middle to make each into a rough square.
3 Dip the crêpe parcels first in the beaten egg, then in the breadcrumbs, coating each one well.
4 Fill a saucepan or deep-frier no more than half-full with oil and place over a high heat. Once the oil reaches 180°C/350°F – when bubbles form on the handle of a wooden spoon stirred into the oil – it is ready for deep-frying.
5 Using a slotted spoon, place the crêpe parcels in the hot oil, seamed-side up, and fry until brown and very crisp: 1–2 minutes. Turn them over and briefly fry the other side. Remove the parcels using the slotted spoon, drain well on a plate lined with crumpled kitchen paper, and serve at once.

VEGETABLE FRITTATA

More substantial than an omelette, a frittata consists of a thick layer of lightly cooked vegetables set with egg in a frying pan and served flat. Similar dishes are found in Spain and the Middle East; frittata is the Italian version. Use any vegetables you like: asparagus and artichoke heart are possibilities. Frittata needs only a salad to accompany it, and can be served cold or warm. Illustrated on pages 100–1. Serves 2.

INGREDIENTS

125g (4oz) baby carrots, trimmed
125g (4oz) shallots, sliced
125g (4oz) courgettes, cut into 6mm (¼in) slices
125g (4oz) mangetout, trimmed
4 free-range eggs
30g (1oz) freshly grated Parmesan cheese
salt and freshly ground black pepper
30ml (2 tbsps) olive oil

PREPARATION

1 Pour a little water (about 5cm/2in deep) into a saucepan and bring to the boil. Add the carrots and shallots, cover and cook for 2 minutes. Add the courgettes and cook for another minute, then the mangetout and cook for 1 minute more. Drain. The vegetables should be tender but still crunchy.
2 Preheat the grill to moderate.
3 Whisk the eggs lightly, add the Parmesan and season with a little salt and black pepper – remembering that the cheese is already salty.
4 Heat the oil in a large frying pan over a moderate heat. Add the vegetables, using a spatula to distribute them evenly around the pan, then pour in the egg mixture, gently moving the vegetables so the egg runs through them.
5 When the bottom of the frittata is set and golden brown (1–2 minutes), put the pan under the grill until the top is set: 1–2 minutes. Slide it on to a plate and serve, cut in half or in wedges.

SPINACH TIMBALES

Eggs, cream and spinach, set in small dariole moulds or cups, make a light and delicious first course. Illustrated on page 100. Serves 6 as a starter.

INGREDIENTS

butter and dry grated Parmesan to coat the moulds
15g (½oz) butter
250g (8oz) frozen chopped spinach
4 free-range eggs
150ml (5fl oz) single cream
60ml (4 tbsps) double cream
freshly grated nutmeg
salt and freshly ground black pepper
torn frisée and carrot knots (page 145) to garnish, optional

PREPARATION

1 Preheat the oven to 160°C/325°F/gas 3. Line the bases of 6 x 150ml (5fl oz) dariole moulds or cups with circles of nonstick paper, grease with butter and dust with dry Parmesan.
2 Melt the butter in a large saucepan over a moderate heat, add the spinach, cover and cook until the spinach is tender: 3–4 minutes.
3 Separate two of the eggs. Place the yolks in a bowl (reserve the whites to use in another recipe), add the two whole eggs and the cream, and beat.
4 Pour the egg and cream mixture into the pan with the spinach, mix well, and season with nutmeg, salt and black pepper. Divide among the prepared moulds. Bake in a bain-marie (see page 147) until set and firm to the touch and a skewer inserted into the centre comes out clean: 30–35 minutes.
5 Timbales can be served while still warm or when cool. Allow to cool slightly – or completely – then loosen the sides with a knife and turn each one out on to a small plate. Garnish with a little torn frisée and carrot knots if wished, and serve.

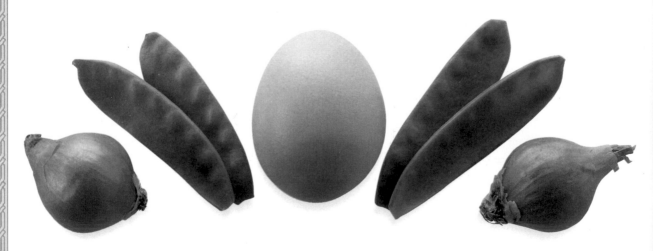

CLASSIC OMELETTE

Use the best free-range eggs you can find for an excellent, highly satisfying omelette. Illustrated (with fresh herbs) on page 15. Serves 1.

INGREDIENTS

*2 free-range eggs
salt and freshly ground black pepper
15g (½oz) butter*

PREPARATION

1 Break the eggs into a bowl and beat them lightly until yolks and whites have just combined. Season with salt and black pepper.
2 Place a small frying pan (about 15cm/6in across the base) over a moderate heat and, when it is hot, put in the butter. Swirl the butter around the pan without letting it brown. Pour in the eggs, tipping the pan so that it is evenly coated.
3 Using a fork, draw the edges of the egg towards the centre and let the liquid egg run to the edges. Repeat until the omelette is almost set but still a little moist on top – it takes around a minute. Add the filling, fold the omelette into three (see page 148), serve, and eat at once.

SOUFFLE OMELETTE

Halfway between a soufflé and an omelette, this is far quicker to cook than a soufflé, and makes a change from a classic omelette. Serves 1.

INGREDIENTS

*2 free-range eggs, separated
30ml (2 tbsps) cold water
salt and freshly ground black pepper
15g (½oz) butter*

PREPARATION

1 Preheat the grill to moderate.
2 Put the egg yolks and water into a large bowl, season and mix well.
3 In a separate greasefree bowl, whisk the egg whites until they stand in soft peaks.
4 Using a metal spoon, stir a little egg white into the yolks, then fold in the rest of the egg white.
5 Follow step 2 of the Classic omelette, above.
6 After 1–2 minutes, when the bottom of the omelette is set and golden brown, put the pan under the grill and brown the top: 1–2 minutes.
7 Slit the omelette open without cutting right through the base (this makes it foldable). Spoon your chosen filling over it, fold it and serve.

OMELETTE FILLINGS

A basic omelette, whether classic or soufflé, can have a wide variety of fillings, both sweet and savoury. Each of the suggestions below is for a savoury omelette, and serves 1. For sweet omelettes, add fruit or jam of your choice and, if desired, a dusting of icing sugar. Have the filling ready to spoon on to the omelette the moment the omelette is cooked; then fold and serve.

ASPARAGUS Trim 2 – 4 asparagus spears and place in a frying pan. Pour in a little boiling water, cover and half-boil, half-steam them until tender: 3–4 minutes. Cut into 2.5cm (1in) lengths.
RED PEPPER Grill and peel half a pepper (as shown on page 144) then slice the flesh.
MUSHROOM Slice 60g (2oz) mushrooms – any type, or a mixture – and sauté in 15g (½oz) butter until they are tender and any liquid has evaporated: 5–15 minutes, depending on how much liquid they make. Season with salt and black pepper.
TRUFFLE Shave some black truffle on to the freshly cooked omelette and fold the omelette straight away.
RATATOUILLE Ratatouille (page 62) makes a good omelette filling: gently reheat about 2 generous tablespoons.
CHEESE Stir 2 tablespoons of grated cheese into the beaten eggs, then sprinkle 2 more tablespoons (of a different cheese, if desired) on to the freshly cooked omelette just before folding it. Gruyère and Parmesan are both delicious.
ARTICHOKE Allow 1–2 artichoke bases per person, prepared as shown on page 146, then sliced and gently tossed in a frying pan with 15g (½oz) melted butter until tender.
ROCKET This is a good filling if you like strong flavours. Use 60g (2oz) of leaves, added either raw or after being cooked in 2 teaspoons of olive oil in a frying pan for 1–2 minutes.
PEAS & MINT Cover 60g (2oz) fresh or frozen peas with boiling water and cook until tender: about 2 minutes. Drain and add a small knob of butter and 2 teaspoons of chopped mint.

*Spinach timbale
(page 98)*

*Light bread rolls
(page 103)*

*Vegetable frittata
(page 98)*

BREAD, PIZZAS & PASTRY

Fresh, home-baked breads and pastries are universally popular and an important part of the vegetarian diet. Flans and pies, in all their variety, make excellent, substantial main courses as well as delicious food for parties, picnics and summer meals outdoors. Two of the dishes in this section, the gougère and the cashew and tomato pâté en croûte, make stunning centrepieces for special dinners, while the easy yeast-based dough for light bread rolls and authentic pizza bases is the stuff of delicious everyday meals.

QUICK & EASY BROWN BREAD

This bread is made by the quick, one-rise method, which does not require any kneading. The dough is mixed, put into the tin to rise, then baked. Use fresh or dried yeast – I prefer fresh, it is pleasant to handle and seems to work more quickly. Two things are important: that the yeast is not stale (whether fresh or dried), and that the dough is not allowed to get hot until it goes into the oven. Makes two 500g (1lb) loaves or one 1kg (2lb) loaf.

INGREDIENTS

*500g (1lb) plain strong wholemeal flour
2 tsps salt
15g (½oz) fresh yeast **or** 2 tsps dried yeast
1 tsp sugar
400ml (13fl oz) tepid (not warm or hot) water
butter or olive oil to grease the tin*

PREPARATION

1 Tip the flour and salt into a large bowl, mix roughly with your fingers and then leave in a warm place, such as an oven on very low, until the flour is warm to the touch. It is important that the flour does not get hot, it should be only warm.
2 If using fresh yeast, crumble it into a small bowl with the sugar and pour in 150ml (5fl oz) of the tepid water. If using dried yeast, put 150ml (5fl oz) of the water and the sugar into the bowl first, then sprinkle the yeast on top and stir.
3 Leave the yeast until it has frothed up like the head on a glass of beer: about 5 minutes.

4 Generously grease two 500g (1lb) loaf tins or one large 1kg (2lb) tin with butter or olive oil.
5 Add the yeast to the flour and enough of the remaining tepid water to make a fairly soft mixture that leaves the sides of the bowl clean. Add a little more tepid water if necessary.
6 Halve the dough if necessary. Flatten the dough into a rectangle, gently roll it up to fit the tin, and place it into the tin with the fold underneath. Push the dough down into the sides and corners of the tin to give a domed shape to the bread.
7 Cover the tin(s) with clingfilm or a clean tea towel wrung out in hot water and leave in a warm place (such as near a radiator or in an airing cupboard) until the dough is within 6mm (¼in) of the top of the tin: about 30 minutes if the room is reasonably warm, longer – up to an hour perhaps – if the room is cool.
8 Preheat the oven to 200°C/400°F/gas 6.
9 Bake the bread until it is brown and firm to the touch: about 45 minutes for one loaf, 35 minutes for two. The bread should sound hollow when slipped out of the tin and tapped on the base with your knuckles. To crisp the base and sides more, return the loaf to the oven for a few minutes after removing it from the tin. Cool on a wire rack.

VARIATION

For a lighter loaf, replace up to half the wholemeal flour with strong white flour. Mix the flours roughly together in the bowl with your fingers, and then make the bread in exactly the same way as the all wholemeal version.

LIGHT BREAD ROLLS

This olive oil dough requires a little kneading. The rolls can be any shape or size: see illustration on page 101.

INGREDIENTS

*175g (6oz) plain strong white flour
175g (6oz) plain strong wholemeal flour
½ tsp salt
15g (½oz) fresh yeast or 2 tsps dried yeast
1 tsp sugar
200ml (7fl oz) tepid water
45ml (3 tbsps) olive oil
butter or oil to grease the baking sheet
beaten egg or milk to glaze, optional
flour, poppy or sesame seeds, or oat flakes to
garnish, optional*

PREPARATION

1 Tip the flours and salt into a large bowl, mix roughly together with your fingers and leave in a warm place until warm (not hot) to the touch.
2 If using fresh yeast, crumble it into a small bowl with the sugar and pour in the tepid water. If using dried yeast, put the water and sugar into the bowl first, then sprinkle the yeast on top and stir.
3 Leave the yeast until it has frothed up like the head on a glass of beer: about 5 minutes.
4 Add the oil to the flour, and pour in the yeast. Mix to a dough that leaves the sides of the bowl clean, then turn it out on to a clean work surface and knead for 5 – 10 minutes or until the dough feels smooth and silky. If sticky, add more flour.
5 Return the dough to the bowl and cover with clingfilm or a clean tea towel wrung out in hot water. Leave in a warm place until the dough has almost doubled in size: 30 minutes to an hour.
6 Punch down the dough with your fist, remove it from the bowl and knead it briefly. Divide it into the required number of pieces and make the roll shapes (see right). Place well apart on a lightly greased baking sheet, cover with clingfilm or a tea towel wrung out in hot water and leave in a warm place until doubled in size: 30 – 60 minutes or more. The rolls should look puffy.
7 Preheat the oven to 200°C/400°F/gas 6.
8 If desired, glaze the rolls with egg or milk and dust with flour or sprinkle with seeds or oat flakes. Bake until the rolls are lightly browned and sound hollow when tapped on the base: about 20 minutes. Cool on a wire rack.

ROLL SHAPES

Rolls can be made in small versions of traditional bread shapes:
KNOT Divide the dough into eight pieces, roll each piece into a thin sausage shape and tie into a loose knot.
COTTAGE Divide the dough into eight pieces and divide two of these into thirds, making six large pieces and six small. Gently roll under the palm of your hand into rounds, then place a small round on top of each large one and push a hole down through the middle of both pieces using the handle of a wooden spoon.
CLOVER LEAF Divide the dough into small pieces: about 18 of them. Roll gently into rounds and place them in threes, touching each other, on the baking sheet. Each group of three – each clover leaf – should be well separated from the next.
PLAIT Divide the dough into three pieces. Divide each piece into three more pieces and roll into long thin sausage shapes. Pinch three ends together, loosely plait, then pinch the other ends together. Tuck the ends under to hold the plait firmly. Repeat to make two more.
BLOOMER Divide the dough into six pieces. Flatten each piece and roll it up like a Swiss roll. Pull down on the ends and tuck them underneath to make the top round and smooth. After the dough has doubled in size and before it is glazed, cut two diagonal slits in the top.

PIZZA BASE

Use the same dough as for the light bread rolls, left. Makes one 30cm (12in) round pizza base or four 15cm (6in) bases. A selection of toppings appears on page 104.

PREPARATION

1 Follow steps 1 to 5 of the recipe on the left.
2 Lightly grease a pizza plate or baking sheet with butter or olive oil.
3 Punch down the dough with your fist, remove it from the bowl and knead it briefly. Flatten it into a circle 30cm (12in) in diameter or, to make individual pizzas, divide the dough into four pieces and flatten these into circles 15cm (6in) in diameter. Place on the plate or baking sheet.
4 Arrange the toppings and bake the pizza or pizzas in the preheated oven as described overleaf.

ASPARAGUS, ROCKET & PARMESAN PIZZA

Makes one 30cm (12in) pizza.

INGREDIENTS

200g (7oz) asparagus tips
60g (2oz) rocket leaves, lightly torn
1 x 30cm (12in) pizza base (page 103), uncooked
olive oil, to taste
salt and freshly ground black pepper
60g (2oz) Parmesan cheese, flaked

PREPARATION

1 Preheat the oven to 200°C/400°F/gas 6.
2 Cook the asparagus in boiling water until just tender: 2–3 minutes.
3 Strew the rocket over the pizza base. Arrange the asparagus on top like the spokes of a wheel. Brush well with oil and season to taste.
4 Bake for 10 minutes. Add the cheese, return to the oven and bake until crisp at the edges and light brown on top: 10 minutes. Serve at once.

ARTICHOKE, AVOCADO & OYSTER MUSHROOM PIZZA

Makes one 30cm (12in) pizza.

INGREDIENTS

30ml (2 tbsps) olive oil
175g (6oz) oyster mushrooms
1 quantity basic or fresh tomato sauce (page 121)
1 x 30cm (12in) pizza base (page 103), uncooked
125g (4oz) artichoke hearts, preserved in oil
1 ripe avocado
15ml (1 tbsp) lemon juice
salt and freshly ground black pepper

PREPARATION

1 Preheat the oven to 200°C/400°F/gas 6.
2 Warm the oil in a pan over a moderate heat, add the mushrooms and fry for 5 minutes.
3 Spread the tomato sauce over the pizza base. Drain the artichoke hearts, reserving the oil, slice them and arrange with the mushrooms over the pizza. Brush well with the oil that the artichokes were preserved in. Bake for 15 minutes.
4 Halve the avocado, remove the peel and stone and slice the flesh; sprinkle with the lemon juice.
5 Remove the pizza from the oven, arrange the avocado on top, season and return to the oven for 5 more minutes. Serve at once.

AUBERGINE, RED ONION & GREEN OLIVE PIZZA

Makes one 30cm (12in) pizza.

INGREDIENTS

1 large aubergine, cut into 2.5 x 5cm (1 x 2in) strips
2 red onions, sliced
olive oil, to drizzle
1 x 30cm (12in) pizza base (page 103), uncooked
125g (4oz) large green olives
salt and freshly ground black pepper
60g (2oz) goat's cheese, sliced or diced, optional

PREPARATION

1 Preheat the oven to 200°C/400°F/gas 6.
2 Place the aubergine and onion in the grill pan or on a baking sheet. Drizzle oil over them, mix gently with your hands to spread the oil evenly and place under a hot grill until tender and lightly browned: 10–15 minutes, turning with tongs and adding more oil as necessary.
3 Arrange the aubergine and onion over the pizza base, place the olives on top and season well.
4 If adding cheese, bake without the cheese for 10 minutes then add the cheese and return to the oven. Bake until crisp at the edges and light brown on top: 10 more minutes. Alternatively, bake without cheese until crisp at the edges and cooked in the middle: 20 minutes. Serve at once.

INDIVIDUAL PIZZAS

The pizza dough on page 103 makes four individual pizza bases of around 15cm (6in) diameter. Some ingredients lend themselves particularly well to small pizzas: cherry tomatoes for example. Bake at the same temperature as the larger pizzas (200°C/400°F/ gas 6) but for less time: 10–15 minutes.

CHERRY TOMATO PIZZAS Spread fresh tomato sauce (page 121) evenly over the bases. Thinly slice 250g (8oz) red or yellow cherry tomatoes, arrange over the top and season well. Bake until the pizzas are crisp at the edges and cooked in the middle: 10–15 minutes. Serve warm, strewn with fresh basil leaves.

MULTI-COLOURED PEPPERS PIZZAS Take 1 red, 1 yellow and 1 green pepper, quarter, grill and peel them as shown on page 144, and cut the flesh into strips. Arrange over the bases, drizzle with olive oil if liked, and season well. Bake until crisp at the edges and cooked in the middle: 10–15 minutes. Serve warm.

SAVOURY FLANS

*These recipes make one 20cm (8in) flan or
four 10cm (4in) small flans. Illustrated on pages 30–1.*

INGREDIENTS

THE FLAN FILLING
a filling chosen from below
THE FLAN CASES
1 x 20cm (8in) shortcrust pastry case **or**
*4 x 10cm (4in) cases, pre-baked and
"waterproofed" as shown on page 151*
THE CUSTARD
*3 free-range egg yolks
200ml (7fl oz) single cream
freshly grated nutmeg, optional
salt and freshly ground black pepper*

PREPARATION

1 Preheat the oven to 160°C/325°F/gas 3.
2 Prepare the flan filling ingredients as described
below and divide among the pre-baked cases.
3 Make the custard: in a small bowl, beat the egg
yolks and the cream to combine them. Add the
nutmeg, if using, and a good seasoning of salt and
black pepper. Pour the custard into a saucepan,
place over a gentle heat and cook, stirring with a
wooden spoon, until it is thick enough to coat the
back of the spoon.
4 Pour the custard over the ingredients in the
pastry cases. Sprinkle with seeds or nuts if using.
Place in the oven and bake until the filling is set
and golden brown on top: 25–30 minutes.

———— *Flan fillings* ————

LEEK & SESAME Slice 250g (8oz) trimmed
leeks. Cover and cook them slowly, stirring
occasionally, in 30g (1oz) butter until tender and
creamy: about 15 minutes. If the leeks produce
liquid, uncover, turn up the heat and boil it
quickly away. Place the leeks in the pastry case or
cases, then season the custard with nutmeg and
pour it over the leeks. Sprinkle 2 tablespoons of
sesame seeds over the custard and bake. Serve
hot, warm or cold.
BLUE CHEESE & ONION WITH ALMONDS
Cook a medium-sized onion, finely chopped, in
15ml (1 tbsp) olive oil until tender: 5 minutes.
Crumble 60g (2oz) blue cheese, mix with the
onion, and place in the pastry case or cases. Pour
the custard over the onion and cheese, sprinkle
with 2 tablespoons of flaked almonds and bake.
Serve hot, warm or cold.

TINY FLANS & TARTLETS

*I usually pre-bake tiny pastry cases before adding
the fillings, but I don't bother to "waterproof" them
(page 151) since they are so small. These amounts fill
6–8 tiny pastry cases. Illustrated on pages 30–1.*

FETA, ROCKET & SUNDRIED TOMATO TARTLETS
Mix 125g (4oz) diced feta cheese and 12 roughly
torn rocket leaves with 4 sundried tomatoes, cut
into strips. Season with black pepper, divide evenly
among 6–8 pre-baked tartlet cases and serve.
BLACK OLIVE & TOMATO TARTLETS Make a
small quantity of tomato sauce (page 121) and
spoon it into 6–8 pre-baked tartlet cases. Cut
6–8 pitted black olives into strips and arrange
over the sauce. Garnish with sprigs of oregano
and serve.
MIXED PEPPER BARQUETTES Take 1 red and
1 yellow pepper, quarter, grill and peel them as
shown on page 144, and cut the flesh into strips.
Arrange in 6–8 pre-baked barquette cases, garnish
with sprigs of basil and serve.
CHERRY TOMATO BARQUETTES Preheat the
oven to 160°C/325°F/gas 3. Thinly slice 6 cherry
tomatoes and arrange most of the slices in 6–8
pre-baked barquette cases. Mix 1 egg yolk with
45ml (3 tbsps) of single cream and season with salt
and black pepper. Spoon this mixture over the
tomatoes in the cases, garnish with the remaining
tomatoes and bake until the filling is set:
5–10 minutes. Serve warm or cold.
AVOCADO & SPRING ONION TINY FLANS
Preheat the oven to 160°C/325°F/gas 3. Finely
slice 2 small spring onions and fry in a little olive
oil until tender: 3 minutes. Mix 1 egg yolk with
120ml (8 tbsps) single cream and season with salt
and pepper. Peel, stone and slice a small avocado,
mix it with the spring onion and divide among
6 tiny flan cases. Pour in enough of the cream and
egg mixture to fill the cases. Bake until the filling
is set: 5–10 minutes. Serve warm or cold.
CARROT & CARDAMOM TINY FLANS
Preheat the oven to 160°C/325°F/gas 3. Finely
slice 125g (4oz) baby carrots and boil them with
a cardamom pod until tender: about 2 minutes.
Drain the carrots and divide them among the small
flan cases. Split the cardamom pods, scoop out the
seeds and put them in a bowl with 1 egg and
120ml (8 tbsps) cream. Mix the egg with the
cream and season with salt and black pepper. Fill
the cases with the mixture. Bake until the filling is
set: 5–10 minutes. Serve warm or cold.

CASHEW NUT & TOMATO PATE EN CROUTE

A moist cashew nut and tomato pâté with a coat of light flaky puff pastry makes an excellent main course. It is made in two stages: the pâté is baked and cooled, then wrapped in pastry and baked again. Serves 4.

INGREDIENTS

butter, to coat tin
30ml (2 tbsps) sundried tomato oil or olive oil
1 large onion, finely chopped
2 large cloves garlic, finely chopped
400g (14oz) can whole tomatoes, drained and chopped
12 sundried tomatoes in oil, finely chopped
200g (7oz) cashew nuts, finely chopped
rind of ½ lemon, pith removed, rind finely chopped
1 tbsp chopped fresh basil
1 free-range egg, beaten
salt and freshly ground black pepper
250g (8oz) frozen puff pastry or homemade
quick flaky pastry (page 150)

PREPARATION

1 Preheat the oven to 180°C/350°F/gas 4. Line a 500g (1lb) loaf tin with nonstick paper and grease with butter. A shallow tin (5cm/2in deep) is best.
2 Warm the oil in a saucepan over a moderate heat, add the onion and garlic, cover and cook for 5 minutes. Add the tomatoes and cook, uncovered, until any liquid has evaporated: about 3 minutes.
3 Remove from the heat and stir in the sundried tomatoes, cashew nuts, lemon rind, basil and all but 2 teaspoons of the egg (reserve for glazing). Season with salt and black pepper.
4 Spoon the mixture into the tin, smoothing the top. Bake until the centre is firm to the touch: 45–60 minutes. Remove from the heat and allow to cool. Then turn the pâté out of the tin, wrap in foil or clingfilm and cool in the refrigerator.

The pâté can be made in advance and stored in the refrigerator for 2 – 3 days.

5 Preheat the oven to 200°C/400°F/gas 6.
6 On a lightly floured board, roll out the puff pastry to a 30cm (12in) square. Cut off the top third, measuring 30 x 10cm (12 x 4in).
7 Place the pâté on the smaller piece of pastry and drape the larger piece of pastry over the top, covering the pâté completely. Ease the pastry down the sides and press the edges firmly together at the bottom, sealing with water. Trim, make steam holes in the top and glaze with beaten egg.
8 Bake until the pastry is crisp and puffed up: 25–30 minutes. Serve at once.

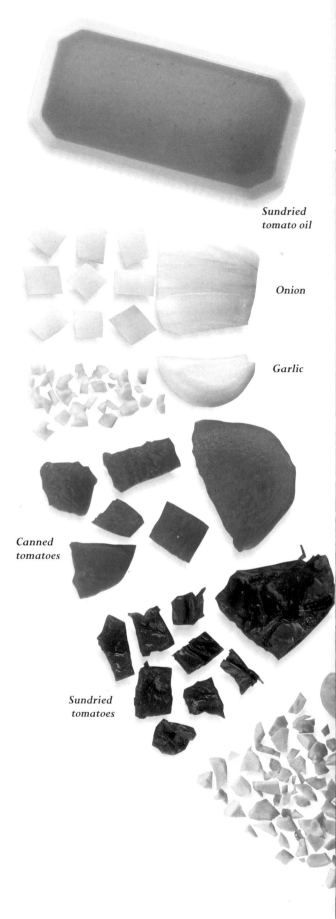

Sundried tomato oil

Onion

Garlic

Canned tomatoes

Sundried tomatoes

Cashew nuts

Lemon rind

Basil

Beaten egg

Salt

Black
pepper

Puff pastry

FLAKY LEEK & POTATO PIE

Satisfyingly creamy leeks and potatoes are baked under a flaky crust, which can be decorated according to your skill and ambition. Serves 4.

INGREDIENTS

750g (1½lb) potatoes, thinly sliced
500g (1lb) trimmed leeks, sliced
30g (1oz) butter
250g (8oz) onions, finely chopped
2 tbsps chopped fresh chives
2 tbsps chopped fresh flat-leaf parsley
400g (14oz) crème fraîche
freshly grated nutmeg
salt and freshly ground black pepper
250g (8oz) frozen puff pastry or homemade quick flaky pastry (page 150)
beaten egg to glaze, optional

PREPARATION

1 Cook the potatoes in boiling water until just tender: 8–10 minutes. In another pan, cook the leeks in boiling water until just tender: 8–10 minutes. Drain. (The water from both vegetables makes good stock.)
2 Melt the butter in a large saucepan over a moderate heat, add the onion, cover and cook until tender: about 10 minutes.
3 Remove the onion from the heat and add the potatoes, leeks, herbs and crème fraîche. Mix well, season with nutmeg, salt and black pepper, and leave to cool.
4 Preheat the oven to 200°C/400°F/gas 6.
5 Take a pie dish of 1.5 litre (2½ pint) capacity. Roll out the pastry so that it is larger all round than the pie dish. Cut around the pie dish to make the pie lid, and then cut around this, 2.5cm (1in) from the dish, to make the pie rim. Set these, and any trimmings, aside.
6 Spoon the filling into the pie dish. It should fill it generously and form a rounded dome.
7 Fit the pastry rim on the edge of the pie dish, pleating it if necessary, brush with cold water and position the pie lid on top to cover the whole dish. Press the edges firmly together to seal, then scallop them as shown on page 151. Make a steam hole in the centre.
8 Decorate the pie with pastry trimmings, sticking them on with cold water, then brush with beaten egg if desired. Bake until puffed up and golden brown: 35–40 minutes. Serve at once.

GRUYERE GOUGERE

A gougère – a circle of golden, light, cheese-enriched choux pastry filled with vegetables cooked in red wine – makes a mouthwatering centrepiece for a meal. Other fillings can be good too: try the braised vegetable recipes on page 62. Serves 4.

INGREDIENTS

THE GOUGERE
60g (2oz) butter, plus extra to coat the dish
90g (3oz) plain flour
2 free-range eggs
90g (3oz) Gruyère cheese, grated
salt and freshly ground pepper
THE FILLING
30g (1oz) butter
15ml (1 tbsp) olive oil
1 large onion, sliced
4 cloves garlic, chopped
250g (8oz) baby carrots
125g (4oz) baby button mushrooms
1 bay leaf
1 sprig of rosemary
300ml (½ pint) red wine
chopped fresh flat-leaf parsley, to garnish

PREPARATION

1 Preheat the oven to 200°C/400°F/gas 6.
2 Put the butter into a medium saucepan with 150ml (5fl oz) of cold water and heat gently to melt the butter and bring the water to the boil.
3 Remove from the heat and sift in the flour. Stir vigorously, then return to the heat and keep stirring until the mixture leaves the sides of the pan. Remove from the heat once again.
4 Add the eggs and beat the mixture with a wooden spoon until it becomes smooth and glossy: 2–3 minutes. Stir in two-thirds of the cheese and season well.
5 Lightly grease a 30cm (12in) ovenproof plate or dish with butter and place spoonfuls of mixture on it in a ring. Sprinkle the rest of the cheese on top. Bake until it has risen, looks golden and is firm to the touch: about 35 minutes.
6 Meanwhile, make the filling. Melt half the butter with the oil in a large pan over a moderate heat, add the onion and fry for 5 minutes. Add the garlic, carrots, mushrooms and herbs and fry for a further 5 minutes, then reduce the heat.
7 Pour in the wine and cook until it has reduced by half: about 20 minutes. Discard the herbs. Season and add the rest of the butter.
8 Spoon the vegetables into the centre of the gougère, sprinkle with parsley and serve at once.

ASPARAGUS FILO FLOWERS

Makes 12. Illustrated on page 18.

INGREDIENTS

filo pastry (see page 150 for tips on using it)
melted butter for brushing
8 asparagus spears, trimmed
1 quantity of hollandaise sauce (page 123)

PREPARATION

1 Preheat the oven to 200°C/400°F/gas 6.
2 You need a bun tin and, for each flower, two squares of filo pastry that are slightly bigger than the cup-shaped hollows. Cut the filo into squares.
3 Brush a little melted butter into each hollow and put in one square of filo pastry, then place another on top slightly askew, so there are eight points sticking up. Brush again with melted butter for an extra-rich result.
4 Continue until the tin is full. Bake the flowers until golden and crisp: about 5 minutes. Remove from the oven and leave to cool.
5 Cut the asparagus spears in three and boil briefly in salted boiling water until tender: about 3 minutes. Allow to cool.
6 Place the flowers on a serving platter, fill each one with a generous amount of hollandaise and arrange two asparagus pieces in it. Serve at once.

VARIATION

FILO FLOWERS WITH BROCCOLI AND TOMATO
Arrange lightly cooked broccoli florets and strips of fresh tomato in hollandaise-filled flowers.

SPRING ROLLS

Makes 12. Illustrated on page 18.

INGREDIENTS

30ml (2 tbsps) olive oil
1 medium-sized onion, finely chopped
1 green pepper, cored, seeded and finely chopped
175g (6oz) button mushrooms, sliced or chopped
300g (10oz) beansprouts
15ml (1 tbsp) soy sauce
freshly ground black pepper
filo pastry (see page 150 for tips on using it)
melted butter for brushing

PREPARATION

1 Warm the oil in a large saucepan over a moderate heat, add the onion and pepper, cover and cook until tender: about 10 minutes.
2 Add the mushrooms and beansprouts and cook uncovered for a further 2–3 minutes. Remove from the heat, add the soy sauce, season with black pepper and leave to cool.
3 Preheat the oven to 200°C/400°F/gas 6.
4 Fold a sheet of filo pastry in half lengthways. Spoon some mixture on to the narrow end of the strip of pastry, make a 1cm (½in) fold like a hem down each side, then roll the package up. Brush with melted butter and place on a baking sheet. Repeat until the filling is used up.
5 Bake until golden and crisp on both sides: after about 20 minutes on one side, turn over and bake for 10–15 minutes on the other. Serve at once or recrisp in a warm oven later.

LEEK PARCELS

Makes 8. Illustrated on page 18.

INGREDIENTS

500g (1lb) potatoes, finely diced
350g (12oz) trimmed leeks, finely sliced
150ml (5fl oz) single cream
2 tbsps chopped fresh flat-leaf parsley
salt and freshly ground black pepper
filo pastry (see page 150 for tips on using it)
melted butter for brushing

PREPARATION

1 Cook the potatoes and leeks in boiling water in separate pans until just tender: 5–6 minutes each. Drain. (The water makes good stock.)
2 Put the potatoes and leeks into a bowl and pour in the cream, adding a little at a time so that you can prevent the mixture becoming too runny. Stir in the flat-leaf parsley, season with salt and black pepper and mix well.
3 Preheat the oven to 200°C/400°F/gas 6.
4 Cut a sheet of filo pastry in half lengthwise and arrange one piece on top of the other in a cross shape. Place some filling in the centre and fold over the four flaps to make a parcel. Brush with melted butter and place on a baking sheet. Repeat until the filling is used up.
5 Bake until golden and crisp on both sides: after about 20 minutes on one side, turn them over and bake for 10–15 minutes longer on the other. Serve at once or recrisp in a warm oven later.

SPICED VEGETABLE TRIANGLES

Makes 8. Illustrated on page 19.

INGREDIENTS

15ml (1 tbsp) olive oil
1 medium-sized onion, finely chopped
½ tsp grated fresh ginger
½ tsp cumin seeds
½ tsp ground coriander
100g (3½oz) finely diced potato
100g (3½oz) finely diced carrot
100g (3½oz) frozen peas
2 tbsps chopped fresh coriander
salt and freshly ground black pepper
filo pastry (see page 150 for tips on using it)
melted butter for brushing

PREPARATION

1 Warm the oil in a large pan over a moderate heat, add the onion, cover and cook until tender: 5 minutes. Add the spices, potato and carrot, cover and cook until the vegetables are tender: 5 – 10 minutes. Stir occasionally, and add a tablespoon or so of water if the mixture sticks.
2 Put in the frozen peas and stir until they are thawed. Add the fresh coriander and seasoning.
3 Preheat the oven to 200°C/400°F/gas 6.
4 Cut a sheet of filo pastry lengthways into two strips. Spoon filling on to the top edge of one strip and make a triangle as shown above. Brush with melted butter, place on a baking sheet and repeat.
5 Bake until golden and crisp: about 15 minutes.

MONEY BAGS

Makes 12. Illustrated on page 19.

INGREDIENTS

125g (4oz) ricotta cheese
30g (1oz) freshly grated Parmesan cheese
filo pastry (see page 150 for tips on using it)
melted butter for brushing

PREPARATION

1 Preheat the oven to 200°C/400°F/gas 6.
2 Mix together the ricotta and Parmesan cheese.
3 Cut the filo into 12cm (5in) squares. Brush one square with melted butter and place another on top slightly askew. Spoon filling on to the middle and gather up the edges, pressing them together to make a pouch. Brush with melted butter, place on a baking sheet and repeat.
4 Bake until golden and crisp: about 5 minutes.

MAKING A FILO TRIANGLE

1 Place the filling at the top of the pastry strip and draw one corner diagonally across to make a triangle.

LITTLE GREEK PIES

Makes 8. Illustrated on page 19.

INGREDIENTS

125g (4oz) frozen spinach
15ml (1 tbsp) olive oil
1 medium-sized onion, finely chopped
½tsp fennel seeds
60g (2oz) feta cheese, crumbled or diced
salt and freshly ground black pepper
filo pastry (see page 150 for tips on using it)
melted butter for brushing

PREPARATION

1 Place the spinach in a small pan and cook over a moderate heat until thawed and any water has evaporated: 2 – 3 minutes. Drain, squeezing out excess water, and transfer to a bowl.
2 Warm the oil in a pan over a moderate heat, add the onion, cover and cook for 5 minutes. Add the fennel seeds and cook for 1 – 2 minutes longer.
3 Add the onion mixture and the feta cheese to the spinach. Season lightly with salt (remembering that feta cheese is already salty) and black pepper, mix thoroughly and allow to cool.
4 Preheat the oven to 200°C/400°F/gas 6.
5 Cut a sheet of filo pastry lengthways into two strips. Spoon filling on to the top edge of one strip and make a triangle as shown above. Brush with melted butter, place on a baking sheet and repeat.
6 Bake until golden and crisp: about 10 minutes.

 Filo parcels and pies are best served straight from the oven. If made in advance, they can be recrisped in a warm oven before serving.

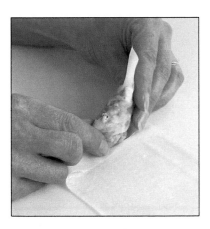

2 Begin to wrap the filling into a parcel by carefully folding the triangle over at its base.

3 Continue to wrap the parcel until you get to the end of the strip. Trim off any spare pastry.

4 Brush with melted butter, making sure the edges of the triangle are well sealed. Place on a baking sheet.

Greek pies

GRAINS & PULSES

Many of the world's most celebrated dishes have as their base one of the rich variety of grains and pulses available. Their international use is reflected in the classic recipes here, ranging from India's dal and Italy's risotto to "new wave" red bean roulade and a saffron-infused vegetable version of Spain's paella.

RICE & AUBERGINE MOULD

*This looks impressive made in a large
(1 litre / 1¾ pint) mould, and can also be made in six
individual moulds such as timbales. Serves 6.*

INGREDIENTS

*300g (10oz) brown rice
2 medium-sized aubergines, thinly sliced
30ml (2 tbsps) olive oil, plus extra for
frying the aubergines and greasing the mould
1 large onion, chopped
1 red pepper, deseeded and chopped
2 cloves garlic, chopped
¼ tsp chilli powder
2 large tomatoes, peeled and chopped
4 tbsps chopped fresh flat-leaf parsley
salt and freshly ground black pepper
sprigs of fresh basil, to garnish*

PREPARATION

1 First, cook the rice (page 152). Remove from the heat but leave the pan covered.
2 Prepare the aubergines. For a rich result, shallow fry in olive oil until tender: 2–3 minutes each side. Drain well on kitchen paper to remove excess oil. For a less rich result, steam until just tender: 4–5 minutes. Put on one side.
3 Warm 30ml (2 tbsps) of olive oil over a moderate heat, add the onion and red pepper, cover and cook for 10 minutes. Add the garlic, chilli powder, tomatoes and cook, uncovered, until the tomatoes have reduced: about 10 minutes.
4 Add the tomato mixture to the rice, along with the parsley and salt and black pepper. Mix well.
5 Brush the mould(s) with oil and arrange the aubergine to cover the surface completely. Spoon in the rice mixture, pressing down firmly, and top with any remaining aubergine slices.
6 Place in the refrigerator to serve chilled, or cover with foil and transfer to a warm oven. Turn out on a large plate, garnish with basil and serve.

MIXED VEGETABLE PILAU

*This is a spiced rice dish that goes well with Bombay
potatoes and Spiced okra (page 86). Serves 4.*

INGREDIENTS

*45ml (3 tbsps) olive oil
1 medium-sized onion, chopped
250g (8oz) carrots, diced
2 cloves garlic, chopped
1 bay leaf
½ cinnamon stick
4 cardamom pods, crushed
2 tsps cumin seeds
350g (12oz) long-grain brown or white rice
salt
125g (4oz) frozen peas, thawed
250g (8oz) button mushrooms, sliced
freshly ground black pepper
chopped fresh coriander, to serve*

PREPARATION

1 Warm 30ml (2 tbsps) of the oil in a large saucepan over a moderate heat, add the onion and carrots, cover and cook for 10 minutes. Stir in the garlic, bay leaf and spices.
2 Add the rice, 900ml (1½ pints) of water and 1 teaspoon of salt. Bring to the boil, then reduce the heat, cover and cook until the rice is done: 40 minutes for brown rice, 20 for white. The dish should be moist but not runny when cooked.
3 Place the peas on top of the rice, cover the pan and take it off the heat. Let it stand for 10 minutes to finish cooking in its own heat.
4 Meanwhile, fry the mushrooms in the remaining oil until they are tender and any liquid they produce has evaporated: 5–10 minutes.
5 Add the mushrooms to the rice mixture. Stir gently with a wooden fork to combine all the ingredients, removing and discarding the bay leaf and cinnamon stick if desired. Season to taste and serve, sprinkled with coriander.

VEGETABLE PAELLA

This is a vegetable version of the classic Spanish dish. Vary the vegetables as much as you like, but put quick-cooking ones, such as courgettes, on top of the rice towards the end of the cooking time. Traditionally this dish is flavoured and coloured with saffron. Turmeric, which is similar in colour, can be used instead. Serves 4.

INGREDIENTS

*6 saffron threads **or** ¼tsp turmeric (see note above)*
60ml (4 tbsps) olive oil
2 large onions, chopped
250g (8oz) carrots, sliced
1 green and 1 red pepper, deseeded and sliced
1 aubergine, diced
2 cloves garlic, chopped
350g (12oz) short-grain rice
400g (14oz) can whole peeled tomatoes,
coarsely chopped, with juice
salt and freshly ground black pepper
chopped fresh flat-leaf parsley, to serve

PREPARATION

1 If you are using saffron, put the threads into a jug and fill with 300ml (½ pint) boiling water. Leave to soak for 20 minutes.

2 Warm the olive oil in a large saucepan over a moderate heat, add the onions, cover and cook until tender: about 10 minutes.

3 Stir in the carrots, peppers, aubergine, garlic and rice and keep stirring over the heat until the rice becomes translucent: 3–4 minutes.

4 Pour in the tomatoes. Add the saffron together with its soaking water, or the turmeric along with 300ml (½ pint) boiling water, and stir well to mix. Season with plenty of salt – about 2 teaspoons – and some black pepper.

5 Bring the mixture to the boil, then reduce the heat and simmer, covered, until the rice is cooked and the water absorbed: about 20 minutes. Take the paella off the heat and leave to stand, still covered, for 10 more minutes. Check the seasoning and serve, sprinkled with parsley.

BULGUR & PINENUT PILAF

*This light dish of bulgur wheat, nuts and dried fruit
is a popular Turkish meal. Bulgur wheat, which
is quicker to cook than rice, makes a good
accompaniment in place of rice. Serves 4.*

INGREDIENTS

*15g (½oz) butter
15ml (1 tbsp) olive oil
1 medium-sized onion, chopped
2 garlic cloves, chopped
250g (8oz) bulgur wheat
1 tsp sea salt
60g (2oz) pinenuts
60g (2oz) raisins or sultanas, optional
chopped fresh flat-leaf parsley, to serve
freshly ground black pepper*

PREPARATION

1 Melt the butter with the oil in a large saucepan
over a moderate heat, add the onion, cover and
cook for 5 minutes.
2 Stir in the garlic and bulgur wheat, coating the
wheat with the oil and onion, then pour in 600ml
(1 pint) of boiling water and the salt. Return to
the boil, cover and cook until the bulgur wheat is
tender and the water absorbed: about 15 minutes.
3 Meanwhile, spread the pinenuts out in the grill
pan and lightly toast under a hot grill, shaking the
pan to move them around. They toast quickly.
4 Add the nuts, raisins and parsley to the bulgur
wheat, mixing them gently with a fork. Taste,
season with black pepper and serve.

PORCINI RISOTTO

*Italian dried mushrooms – porcini – give this risotto its
distinctive flavour. Other ingredients can be added too:
baby peas and whole baby artichokes are good mixed into
the risotto at the end of the cooking time, and you can
replace 150ml (5fl oz) of the water with the same
volume of dry white wine, added at step 3 along with the
porcini. The dish should be creamy and moist but
with some bite still left in the grains of rice – this is
most easily achieved using arborio rice. Serves 4.*

INGREDIENTS

*10g (just under ½oz) porcini
60ml (4 tbsps) olive oil
2 large onions, chopped
2 garlic cloves, chopped
350g (12oz) arborio, or risotto, rice
300g (10oz) oyster mushrooms
15g (½oz) butter
freshly grated nutmeg
salt and freshly ground black pepper
chopped fresh flat-leaf parsley, to serve*

PREPARATION

1 Put the porcini into a small bowl and cover with
boiling water. Leave to soak.
2 Warm 45ml (3 tbsps) of the oil in a large
saucepan over a moderate heat, add the onions,
cover and cook for 10 minutes. Add the garlic and
rice and stir over the heat for a few minutes until
the rice is well coated in oil and looks translucent.
3 Drain the porcini through a sieve lined with a
filter paper to catch any grit, reserving the liquid.
Make the soaking liquid up to 1 litre (1¾ pints)
with water, pour into a small saucepan and set
over a moderate heat next to the large saucepan.
4 Chop the porcini and stir into the rice. Add the
porcini liquid, a ladleful at a time, stirring each
addition and allowing it to become absorbed
before adding the next. Continue until the risotto
is creamy and the rice *al dente*: about 20 minutes.
5 Meanwhile, fry the oyster mushrooms in the
remaining oil and the butter until they are tender:
about 4 minutes. Stir gently into the rice mixture.
Add nutmeg, salt and black pepper and serve,
sprinkled with parsley.

WILD RICE

*The colours and textures of wild rice mixed with brown
rice and basmati make an attractive side dish. Serves 4.*

INGREDIENTS

*125g (4oz) brown rice
60g (2oz) wild rice
¼ tsp sea salt
60g (2oz) basmati rice*

PREPARATION

1 Put the brown and wild rice in a saucepan with
450ml (¾ pint) water and the salt. Bring to the
boil, cover, reduce the heat and cook until the rice
is tender and the water absorbed: 40 minutes.
2 Cook the basmati rice in plenty of boiling
water: 10 minutes. Drain; rinse with hot water.
3 Mix the rices together with a wooden fork.

LEMON RICE

Refreshing to look at as well as to eat, lemon rice goes well with many dishes. Serves 4.

INGREDIENTS

250g (8oz) long-grain brown or white rice, rinsed
½ tsp turmeric
¼ tsp sea salt
juice and finely sliced rind of ½ lemon
freshly ground black pepper

PREPARATION

1 Put the rice in a saucepan with 600ml (1 pint) water, the turmeric and salt. Bring to the boil.
2 Turn the heat down to very low, cover and cook until the rice is tender and the water absorbed: 40 minutes for brown rice, 20 for white.
3 Add the lemon juice and rind and stir with a wooden fork. Season to taste with black pepper.

HERB RICE

This summery rice goes well with braised vegetable dishes such as ratatouille. It is also good cold. Serves 4.

INGREDIENTS

250g (8oz) long-grain brown or white rice, rinsed
¼ tsp sea salt
6 tbsps finely chopped fresh herbs, such as parsley, mint, chives, tarragon
freshly ground black pepper

PREPARATION

1 Put the rice in a saucepan with 600ml (1 pint) water and the salt. Bring to the boil.
2 Turn the heat down to very low, cover and cook until the rice is tender and the water absorbed: 40 minutes for brown rice, 20 for white.
3 Add the herbs and stir with a wooden fork. Season to taste with black pepper.

COCONUT RICE

This has a smooth texture and a slightly sweet flavour that goes well with spiced vegetable dishes. Serves 4.

INGREDIENTS

250g (8oz) long-grain brown or white rice, rinsed
¼ tsp sea salt
60g (2oz) creamed coconut, cut into flakes
freshly ground black pepper

PREPARATION

1 Put the rice in a saucepan with 600ml (1 pint) water and the salt. Bring to the boil.
2 Add the coconut, turn the heat down to very low, cover and cook until the rice is tender and the water absorbed: 40 minutes for brown rice, 20 for white.
3 Stir gently with a wooden fork. Season to taste with black pepper.

SPICED RICE

Slender basmati rice is available in brown and white varieties; I prefer the nutty taste of brown. Serves 4.

INGREDIENTS

250g (8oz) basmati rice, rinsed
1 bay leaf
spices: ½ cinnamon stick, 2–3 crushed cardamom pods, 1 tsp cumin seeds
¼ tsp sea salt
freshly ground black pepper

PREPARATION

1 Put the rice in a saucepan with 600ml (1 pint) water, the bay leaf, spices and salt. Bring to the boil.
2 Turn the heat down to very low, cover and cook until the rice is tender and the water absorbed: 20 minutes for brown rice, 10–12 for white.
3 Season to taste with black pepper.

RED BEAN ROULADE WITH SOURED CREAM FILLING

The base for this unusual roulade contains neither eggs nor cheese. For a vegan version, replace the cream and curd cheese filling with avocado sauce (page 123). Indeed, avocado sauce goes so well with red beans that it makes the perfect sauce, whatever the filling. Illustrated on page 37. Serves 6 as a starter, 4 as a main course.

INGREDIENTS

30ml (2 tbsps) olive oil
1 medium-sized onion, chopped
2 red peppers, cored, deseeded and chopped
400g (14oz) can whole peeled tomatoes, coarsely
chopped, with their juice
½tsp chilli powder
2 x 400g (14oz) cans red kidney beans, drained
125g (4oz) soft white breadcrumbs
salt and freshly ground black pepper
THE FILLING
250g (8oz) curd cheese
150ml (5fl oz) soured cream
3 tbsps chopped fresh coriander

PREPARATION

1 Preheat the oven to 200°C/400°F/gas 6. Line a 22 x 32cm (9 x 13in) Swiss-roll tin with nonstick paper to extend slightly up the sides.
2 Warm the oil in a large saucepan over a moderate heat, add the onion, cover and cook until tender: 5 minutes. Add the peppers, cover and cook for a further 5 minutes.
3 Add the tomatoes and chilli powder and cook, uncovered, until the excess liquid has evaporated and the mixture is thick: about 15 minutes.
4 Put the beans into a food processor or blender with the tomato mixture and breadcrumbs. Season, then work to a fairly coarse consistency.
5 Spoon the mixture into the tin, spreading it evenly into the corners and levelling the top. Bake in the preheated oven until the centre is firm: 10–15 minutes.
6 Make the filling by beating together the curd cheese, soured cream and coriander.
7 Place a piece of nonstick paper, large enough for the roulade, next to the oven. Remove the roulade from the oven and turn it out, face down, on to the paper. Peel the nonstick paper that was used to line the tin from the top.
8 Spread the filling over the roulade then gently roll it up from one of the narrow edges, pressing it together as you go. Carefully slice the roulade, and serve it on individual plates. It is fragile, and may benefit from reshaping with a palette knife.

RED BEAN CHILLI

A vegetarian chilli is one of the quickest and easiest dishes to make and many people enjoy it. It is ideal for feeding a crowd, too: just double or triple the quantities. At the end of the cooking time, I like to mash the beans a little to make the mixture thick and then serve it with rice, bread or potatoes. Serves 4.

INGREDIENTS

60ml (4 tbsps) olive oil
2 medium-sized onions, chopped
2 red or green peppers, cored, deseeded and chopped
2 fresh green chillies, deseeded and finely chopped
2 cloves garlic, chopped
1 tbsp cumin seeds
2 x 400g (14oz) cans whole peeled tomatoes,
coarsely chopped, with juice
2 x 400g (14oz) cans red kidney beans
salt and freshly ground black pepper

PREPARATION

1 Warm the oil in a large saucepan over a moderate heat, add the onion, cover and cook until tender: 5 minutes. Add the peppers, cover and cook for a further 5 minutes.
2 Add the chillies, garlic and cumin seeds and stir, then pour in the tomatoes.
3 Drain the beans, reserving the liquid. Make the liquid up to 150ml (5fl oz) with water if necessary and pour the beans and liquid into the pan.
4 Bring to the boil, then cover, reduce the heat and cook gently until the mixture is heated through and looks thick: 15–20 minutes. Season to taste with salt and black pepper and serve.

SPINACH DAL

*This dish goes well with Bombay potatoes (page 86),
Spiced rice (page 115) and Spiced okra (page 86).
Serves 4 as a side dish.*

INGREDIENTS

*30ml (2 tbsps) olive oil
2 medium-sized onions, chopped
2 fresh green chillies, deseeded and finely chopped
2 cloves garlic, chopped
2 tsps ground cumin
¼ tsp turmeric
3–4 cardamom pods, crushed
125g (4oz) red lentils
500g (1lb) tender spinach leaves
salt and freshly ground black pepper*

PREPARATION

1 Warm the oil in a large saucepan over a
moderate heat, add the onion, cover and cook for
10 minutes. Stir in the chillies, garlic, cumin,
turmeric and cardamom and cook for 1 minute.
2 Add the lentils and 450ml (15fl oz) of water.
Bring to the boil, then reduce the heat, cover and
cook until the lentils are soft and pale: 20–30
minutes.
3 When the lentils are almost ready, cook the
spinach. Place it in a saucepan with just the water
clinging to its leaves after washing. Cook over a
moderately high heat until wilted and much
reduced in size: about 7 minutes. Drain well.
4 Mix the spinach into the lentil mixture and
season well. Serve at once, or reheat later.

POLENTA

*Coarse or fine cornmeal – polenta – can be pressed into
flat slices, fried in olive oil and served with fresh tomato
sauce (page 121) or tomato salad. Serves 4 as a side dish.*

INGREDIENTS

*250g (8oz) polenta, coarse or fine grain
1 tbsp salt
olive oil for shallow frying
Parmesan cheese and lemon wedges to serve, optional*

PREPARATION

1 Pour the polenta and salt into a medium-sized
saucepan with 1 litre (1¾ pints) of cold water and
mix to a smooth paste. Place over a moderate heat
and stir gently until the mixture boils. Reduce the
heat and cook until the polenta is thick and comes
away from the sides of the pan: about 30 minutes.

2 Spread the mixture on a baking sheet to a
thickness of 1cm (under ½in) and allow to cool.
3 Heat a little olive oil in a frying pan. Cut the
polenta into slices and fry on both sides until crisp
and golden. Drain on kitchen paper. Do not cover
the slices – this makes them soggy – but keep
them warm in the oven if necessary.
4 Serve on a warmed dish, with grated Parmesan
on top and lemon wedges on the side, if desired.

FALAFEL

*This is a quick and easy recipe for falafel, especially if
you have a food processor. To make a light meal, serve
with salad, pitta bread and yogurt mixed with fresh
coriander or dill. Serves 4 as a side dish or snack.*

INGREDIENTS

*400g (14oz) can chickpeas, drained
1 shallot or small onion
1 clove garlic, chopped
½ tsp ground cumin
pinch of cayenne pepper or chilli powder
1 free-range egg, beaten
1 tbsp self-raising flour
salt and freshly ground black pepper
groundnut oil for deep frying
olive oil and lemon juice, to serve*

PREPARATION

1 Put the chickpeas and the shallot or onion into
a food processor and purée. Transfer to a bowl.
Alternatively, put the chickpeas into a bowl, mash
well and then grate the shallot or onion into them.
2 Add the garlic, cumin, cayenne or chilli
powder, egg and flour and mix to make a paste
that just holds together. Season to taste with salt
and black pepper.
3 Pour about 7.5cm (3in) of oil into a saucepan or
deep-frier and place over a high heat. Once the oil
reaches 180°C/350°F – when bubbles form on
the handle of a wooden spoon dipped into the oil
– it is ready.
4 With floured hands, quickly form small
amounts of the chickpea mixture into even
rounds. Use a slotted spoon to place several at a
time into the hot fat. Fry until the submerged part
is crisp – about 1 minute – then turn them over
with the slotted spoon and crisp the other side.
5 Drain the falafel on kitchen paper. Do not cover
– this makes them soggy – but keep them warm in
the oven if necessary.
6 Continue until all the falafel are done. Serve
warm, moistened with olive oil and lemon juice.

Carrot, Courgette & Apricot Couscous

The term "couscous" refers both to the small round semolina-like grains themselves and to the complete dish of cooked grains and stew. The stew varies but is usually lightly spiced and contains chickpeas and perhaps some dried fruit. Serve it with small bowls of relishes with contrasting flavours: diced cucumber, creamy yogurt, toasted almonds, washed and plumped raisins, and shop-bought harissa, a hot pepper sauce. Serves 4.

INGREDIENTS

45ml (3 tbsps) groundnut oil
1 large onion, chopped
250g (8oz) carrots, sliced
2 cloves garlic, chopped
1 tsp ground ginger
¼tsp freshly ground white or black pepper
¼tsp ground cinnamon
125g (4oz) dried apricots, sliced
400g (14oz) can chickpeas, drained
250g (8oz) courgettes, sliced
1½ tsps salt
350g (12oz) couscous
45g (1½oz) butter
chopped flat-leaf parsley, to serve

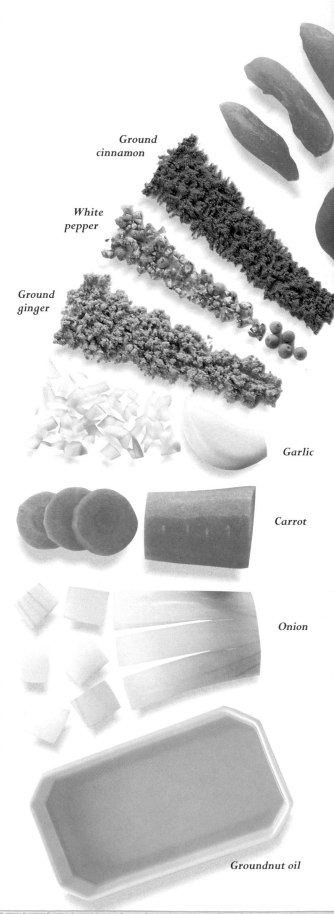

Ground cinnamon

White pepper

Ground ginger

Garlic

Carrot

Onion

Groundnut oil

PREPARATION

1 Heat 2 tablespoons of the oil in a large pan, add the onion and carrots, cover and cook over a moderate heat for 10 minutes.

2 Stir the garlic, ground ginger, white or black pepper and cinnamon into the onion and carrot, cover and cook for 2 minutes.

3 Add the apricots and chickpeas to the pan and pour in 1 litre (1¾ pints) of water. Bring to the boil and simmer until the carrots and apricots are tender and the liquid has reduced and thickened a little: about 20 minutes.

4 Drop in the courgettes, cover and cook until tender: about 10 minutes.

5 Meanwhile, prepare the couscous grain. Put the remaining tablespoon of oil into a large saucepan, pour in 350ml (12fl oz) of water and 1½ teaspoons of salt and place over a high heat. When the water is boiling, take it off the heat, pour in the couscous grain and leave to swell for 2 minutes. Then add the butter, return to the heat and stir with a fork until heated through: 3 minutes.

6 Check the seasoning of the stew, sprinkle with parsley and serve with the couscous.

Chickpeas

Courgette

Salt

Couscous

Butter

Flat-leaf parsley

Dried apricots

SAUCES

A well-chosen sauce adds the finishing touch to both starters and main course dishes. Sauces can look stunning, see the terrines on pages 12–13, for example, and provide just the right touch of piquancy, creaminess, or even sweetness to set off a dish perfectly. In this section, you will find many sauces to enhance your meals. Most are highly versatile and can be made in advance, and all are guaranteed to impress.

PEPPER SAUCE

I like this best made with red peppers, though it works with any colour of pepper. It is a bright, mild but delicious sauce that complements many vegetarian dishes. You can add extra flavourings, as suggested, and use olive oil or butter, depending on the flavour you want. Serves 4.

INGREDIENTS

1 large pepper, cored and deseeded
300ml (½ pint) homemade vegetable stock or water
1 clove garlic, peeled, or a sprig
of thyme, optional
15–30g (½–1oz) butter or
15–30ml (1–2 tbsps) olive oil
salt and freshly ground black pepper
pinch of cayenne pepper or
pinch of chilli powder, optional

PREPARATION

1 Cut the pepper into even-sized chunks and place in a saucepan with the stock or water, and the garlic or thyme if using. Bring to the boil, reduce the heat, cover and simmer until the pepper is tender: about 10 minutes. Remove the garlic or thyme, if used.
2 Pour the pepper and stock or water into a food processor or blender, and purée.
3 Add the butter or oil and blend again.
4 Pass the sauce through a sieve back into the pan (to serve warm) or into a bowl (to serve chilled) and season with salt, black pepper and, if you like, cayenne pepper or chilli powder.
5 Reheat gently and serve warm, or serve chilled from the refrigerator. The sauce can be transferred to a sauceboat or, if preferred, spooned around individual portions on the plates.

Red pepper sauce *Green pepper sauce* *Yellow pepper sauce*

FRESH TOMATO SAUCE

You need a food processor or blender to make this sauce, but it couldn't be easier. Makes 300ml (½ pint).

INGREDIENTS

15ml (1 tbsp) olive oil
1 small onion, finely chopped
1 chopped clove garlic, optional
1kg (2lb) fresh tomatoes, quartered
sea salt

PREPARATION

1 Warm the oil in a large saucepan over a moderate heat, add the onion, and garlic if liked, cover and cook until tender: about 4 minutes.
2 Add the tomatoes and reduce the heat. Cover and cook until the tomatoes have collapsed: about 15 minutes. Take off the heat and allow to cool.
3 Pour the tomatoes into a food processor or blender, and purée. Pass through a sieve back into the pan and season with sea salt. Gently reheat just before serving, or serve cold.

SUNDRIED TOMATO SAUCE

A rich and flavoursome sauce, for which you need a food processor or blender. Makes 300ml (½ pint).

INGREDIENTS

30ml (2 tbsps) oil from the sundried tomatoes
or olive oil
1 small onion, finely chopped
1 chopped clove garlic, optional
400g (14oz) can whole peeled tomatoes,
coarsely chopped, with juice
4 sundried tomatoes in oil
10ml (2 tsps) balsamic vinegar
salt and freshly ground black pepper

PREPARATION

1 Warm the oil (sundried tomato or olive) in a large saucepan over a moderate heat, add the onion, and garlic if using, cover and cook until tender: about 4 minutes.
2 Add the tomatoes and reduce the heat. Cook, uncovered, until any excess liquid has evaporated and the mixture looks thick: about 15 minutes. Take off the heat and leave to cool.
3 Add the sundried tomatoes, pour the mixture into a food processor or blender, and purée. Pass through a sieve back into the pan and add the vinegar. Season to taste and gently reheat before serving, or serve cold.

BASIC TOMATO SAUCE

If you have no fresh tomatoes, or you like a strongly flavoured tomato sauce, try this one. It is ideal for pasta, pizzas, lasagne and other dishes requiring tomato sauce, and is also good as an accompaniment. Makes 300ml (½ pint).

INGREDIENTS

15ml (1 tbsp) olive oil
1 small onion, finely chopped
1 chopped clove garlic, optional
400g (14oz) can whole peeled tomatoes, with juice
sea salt

PREPARATION

1 Warm the oil in a saucepan over a moderate heat, add the onion, and garlic if liked, cover and cook until tender: about 4 minutes.
2 Add the tomatoes and reduce the heat. Cook, uncovered, until any excess liquid has evaporated and the mixture looks thick: about 15 minutes. Take off the heat and allow to cool.
3 Pour the tomatoes into a food processor or blender and purée. Pass through a sieve back into the pan and season with sea salt. Gently reheat just before serving, or serve cold.

RED WINE SAUCE

A delicious, festive sauce. Makes 300ml (½ pint).

INGREDIENTS

60g (2oz) butter
2 shallots, finely chopped
2 tsps finely chopped fresh thyme
1 chopped clove garlic, optional
300ml (½ pint) red wine
45ml (3 tbsps) port or another fortified wine
½ tsp vegetarian bouillon powder
salt and freshly ground black pepper

PREPARATION

1 Melt half the butter in a medium-sized pan over a moderate heat and put the rest of the butter in the refrigerator.
2 Add the shallots and thyme, and garlic if using, to the pan, cover and cook for 5 minutes. Add the wine, port and bouillon powder, season well and bring to the boil. Cook until reduced by half.
3 Cut the butter into small pieces and, just before serving, take the sauce off the heat and whisk in the butter, a little at a time, to make it glossy.

MAYONNAISE

A food processor or blender makes mayonnaise easy to prepare. The handmade version, below, needs more work but is equally successful. Makes 200ml (7fl oz).

INGREDIENTS

2 large free-range egg yolks
¼tsp mustard powder
¼tsp salt
2–3 grindings of black pepper
10ml (2 tsps) white wine vinegar
10ml (2 tsps) lemon juice
200ml (7fl oz) groundnut or light olive oil

PREPARATION

1 Put all the ingredients except the oil into a food processor or blender. Blend at medium speed for 1 minute until everything is well mixed.
2 Turn the speed up to high and start to add the oil, drop by drop, through the top of the machine.
3 When you have added about half, the sound made by the sauce in the blender will change to a "glug-glug". At this point start adding the oil more quickly, pouring it in a thin stream.
4 Taste the sauce and adjust the seasoning if necessary. If the mayonnaise seems too thick, thin it by beating in a teaspoon or two of boiling water. Serve cold. Mayonnaise keeps for up to 5 days, tightly covered, in the refrigerator.

VARIATIONS

HERBED MAYONNAISE Stir 2 – 4 tablespoons of finely chopped fresh herbs into the mayonnaise. Use a mixture of herbs if desired, such as parsley and chives, with a third chosen from coriander, basil, tarragon or mint. Coriander mayonnaise, for example, suits grain and pulse dishes, while tarragon mayonnaise makes a salad very special.
GARLIC MAYONNAISE (AÏOLI) Crush 1 – 4 cloves of garlic and add to the blender with the other ingredients in step 1.

MAKING MAYONNAISE BY HAND

1 Whisk together all the ingredients except the oil. Add half the oil, drop by drop, whisking all the time. A tea towel will prevent the bowl sliding over the worktop while you whisk.

2 The sauce begins to thicken once about half the oil has been added. At this stage, add the oil faster, pouring it in a thin stream while you continue to whisk vigorously.

3 The finished mayonnaise is rich and thick. (If the sauce curdles, the oil was added too quickly. Put an egg yolk in a separate bowl and gradually whisk the curdled mixture into this.)

Stir finely chopped parsley and chives into mayonnaise to create a versatile herbed version. The further addition of basil gives the mayonnaise a particular affinity for tomato-based dishes.

Chives

Parsley

Basil

HOLLANDAISE SAUCE

Like mayonnaise, this is an extremely rich, thickened sauce, but it is served warm rather than cold, and most of its richness comes from butter rather than oil. Serve with steamed asparagus, broccoli, leeks or whole artichokes for a special treat. Makes 200ml (7fl oz).

INGREDIENTS

30ml (2 tbsps) white wine vinegar
250g (8oz) butter
2 large free-range egg yolks
salt and freshly ground black pepper

PREPARATION

1 Put the wine vinegar in a small pan with 45ml (3 tbsps) water, bring to the boil and reduce down to 15ml or a tablespoonful of liquid. Allow to cool.
2 Put the butter into another small pan and heat until foaming.
3 Place the egg yolks and the reduced vinegar in a food processor or blender and blend until combined well.
4 Set the machine running and slowly pour in the butter. As the mixture thickens, add the butter more quickly. Season with salt and pepper. Serve at once or keep warm for a few hours in a vacuum flask or in a bowl over a pan of steaming water.
HANDMADE HOLLANDAISE Reduce the vinegar and water as described in step 1, above. Set a bowl over a pan of gently steaming water on a low heat. Put the egg yolks, reduced vinegar, salt and black pepper into the bowl and whisk until thick and pale: 3 5 minutes. Cut the slightly softened butter (that is, at room temperature) into 6mm (¼in) dice and whisk into the egg yolk mixture a piece at a time. The sauce thickens as the butter is added. Serve the sauce at once or keep it warm in the bowl over the pan of steaming water.

VARIATIONS

MALTAISE SAUCE This is the classic sauce for asparagus. Use the juice of an orange, preferably a blood orange, in place of the vinegar at step 1. Intensify the flavour of the juice by reducing it to 30ml (2 tbsps), then add 1 tablespoon of blanched grated orange peel.
HERBED HOLLANDAISE Stir 2 tablespoons of mixed, chopped fresh herbs into the sauce before serving; parsley, tarragon and chervil make a good combination. Serve with steamed vegetables or a roulade such as Cashew nut and broccoli (page 96).
HOLLANDAISE WITH MUSTARD For a strongly flavoured sauce, add a teaspoon or so of Dijon mustard to the egg yolks at step 1.

BASIL PESTO SAUCE

Homemade pesto is much fresher and more fragrant than the shop-bought variety. Thin with a little warm water for a more pourable sauce. Store, covered, in the refrigerator for up to 5 days. Makes 150ml (5fl oz).

INGREDIENTS

1 clove garlic
30g (1oz) pinenuts or cashew nuts
6 tbsps finely chopped basil leaves
30g (1oz) freshly grated Parmesan cheese
75ml (5 tbsps) olive oil
salt and freshly ground black pepper

PREPARATION

Blend the ingredients into a thick green cream using a food processor or blender.
HANDMADE PESTO Crush the garlic using a pestle and mortar. Add the nuts and crush these to a paste. Add the basil and Parmesan, pound them well, then gradually stir in the olive oil to make a thick green cream.

QUICK HERB SAUCE

This is a quick, fresh-tasting sauce. Makes 200ml (7fl oz).

INGREDIENTS

4 tbsps finely chopped fresh herbs, such as chives or flat-leaf parsley
200ml (7fl oz) crème fraîche or Greek yogurt
salt and freshly ground black pepper

PREPARATION

Stir the herbs into the crème fraîche or yogurt and season to taste. Serve at once or chill in the refrigerator and serve later the same day.

AVOCADO SAUCE

Delicately flavoured yet rich, this sauce is excellent with bean and grain dishes. Makes about 200ml (7fl oz).

INGREDIENTS

1 large ripe avocado pear, halved, stone removed
15 – 30ml (1 – 2 tbsps) lemon juice
salt and freshly ground black pepper

PREPARATION

Spoon the avocado flesh from the skin into a small bowl. Add the lemon juice, season with salt and black pepper and mash well with a fork. Serve the sauce at once; it does not keep.

DESSERTS

Presenting your guests with a fabulous dessert is the way to round off any meal with a flourish. This irresistible selection includes creamy chocolate dishes and unusual sorbets, traditional pies, as well as light, fruit-based desserts, and perfect homemade ice creams.

VANILLA-POACHED PEARS

Choose even-sized, firm pears for this recipe. Poached pears can be served as they are, or with Vanilla ice cream (right) or Chocolate sauce (below). Serves 4.

INGREDIENTS

175g (6oz) caster sugar
rind of ½ lemon, pared in one long strip
1 vanilla pod, split lengthways
300ml (½ pint) water
4 pears, peeled, with stalks intact

PREPARATION

1 Pour the sugar into a saucepan large enough for the pears, and add the lemon rind, vanilla pod and water. Dissolve the sugar over a moderate heat.
2 Put the pears into the liquid, bring the mixture to a gentle simmer, then reduce the heat, cover and leave to cook until the pears are tender right through when pierced with a sharp knife or skewer: 20–30 minutes. Remove from the pan using a slotted spoon and place in a serving dish.
3 Turn up the heat and let the liquid boil until it has reduced a little to make a syrup: about 5 minutes. Discard the rind and pour the syrup, together with the vanilla pod, over the pears. Allow to cool, then refrigerate before serving.

CHOCOLATE SAUCE

INGREDIENTS

250g (8oz) plain chocolate, broken into pieces
60g (2oz) butter
60ml (4 tbsps) water

PREPARATION

1 Place the ingredients in a bowl and set over a saucepan of gently simmering water. Leave until the contents have melted, stirring occasionally.
2 Remove the bowl from the saucepan and beat the contents until smooth and creamy. Serve warm.

VANILLA ICE CREAM

Vanilla sugar enhances the flavour of this ice cream. To make it, break a vanilla pod in half and bury the halves in a jar of sugar. As you use the sugar, top up with more. This ice cream is best eaten within 48 hours. Serves 4.

INGREDIENTS

300ml (½ pint) single cream
1 vanilla pod
4 egg yolks
90g (3oz) sugar, preferably flavoured with a vanilla pod (see note above)
½ tsp vanilla extract
300ml (½ pint) double cream

PREPARATION

1 Put the single cream into a saucepan with the vanilla pod and bring to the boil. Remove from the heat, cover and set aside. This allows the cream to absorb the flavour of the vanilla.
2 Whisk the egg yolks and sugar in a bowl until they become creamy and pale: 2–3 minutes.
3 Reheat the cream to boiling point, then pour it through a sieve on to the egg yolks and sugar and stir well to combine. (Rinse the vanilla pod and dry it; it can be reused many times.)
4 Pour the mixture back into the saucepan and stir it over a low heat until it just thickens and thinly coats the back of a spoon: 2–3 minutes. Be sure to heat it gently to avoid curdling. Stir in the vanilla extract and set the mixture aside to cool.
5 Whip the double cream until it forms soft peaks and fold into the vanilla mixture. Pour into a bowl that will fit the freezer. Freeze until it begins to solidify around the edges: 15–30 minutes.
6 Take out the partially frozen mixture and whisk it well. Return to the freezer for 15–30 minutes, then whisk again. Repeat until the ice cream is too thick to whisk, then leave it to freeze completely.
7 Around 20 minutes before serving, take the ice cream out of the freezer and allow it to soften.

CHOCOLATE & GINGER ROULADE

Rich, creamy and utterly delicious, this is a real treat. Serves 6.

INGREDIENTS

6 large free-range eggs, separated
150g (5oz) caster sugar
60g (2oz) cocoa powder
icing sugar, for dusting
THE FILLING
300ml (½ pint) double cream
60ml (4 tbsps) syrup from the ginger (see below)
4 pieces stem ginger preserved in syrup, finely chopped

PREPARATION

1 Preheat the oven to 190°C/375°F/gas 5. Line a 22 x 32cm (9 x 13in) Swiss-roll tin with nonstick paper.
2 Whisk the egg whites in a greasefree bowl until stiff but not so dry that you can slice them.
3 In another bowl, whisk the egg yolks with the caster sugar until thick and fluffy. Using a metal spoon, fold in the cocoa powder and the egg whites.
4 Pour the mixture into the prepared tin, smoothing it to the edges. Bake until risen and just firm in the centre: about 15 minutes. Leave the roulade base to cool in the tin; it will shrink a great deal. Then turn it out, face down, on to a piece of nonstick paper dusted with icing sugar. Peel the nonstick paper from the top.
5 Prepare the filling. Whip the cream until it forms soft peaks, then whip in the ginger syrup. Stir in the chopped ginger. Spread the cream over the roulade, leaving a 1cm (½in) border all round (to make rolling up easier).
6 Roll up the roulade (see page 95 for the technique). Wrap it in nonstick paper and chill for at least 30 minutes before slicing it. Serve with warm Chocolate sauce (facing page).

DOUBLE-CHOCOLATE BROWNIES WITH HAZELNUTS

These are a chocoholic's delight: they are made from plain chocolate and packed with white chocolate along with toasted hazelnuts. Serve them warm, as a dessert, with crème fraîche or Greek yogurt, or allow them to cool and serve with coffee. Makes 12.

INGREDIENTS

150g (5oz) plain chocolate, at least 50% cocoa solids if possible, broken into pieces
60g (2oz) butter
2 free-range eggs
60g (2oz) brown sugar
60g (2oz) white chocolate, cut into small chips
60g (2oz) hazelnuts, toasted briefly under a hot grill and roughly chopped

PREPARATION

1 Preheat the oven to 180°C/350°F/gas 4. Line a 20cm (8in) square baking tin with nonstick paper.
2 Put the chocolate and butter into a bowl and set over a saucepan of gently simmering water. Leave until melted, stirring occasionally.
3 Meanwhile, break the eggs into a large bowl and add the sugar. Beat the eggs and sugar until they are thick and pale and the trail that the beaters or whisk leave in the mixture remains visible for several seconds. This is very quickly done using an electric whisk at top speed; with a hand whisk it takes around 10 minutes.
4 Pour the melted chocolate and butter mixture on top of the whisked egg mixture and fold it in with a metal spoon, then gently fold in the white chocolate and nuts.
5 Pour this mixture into the tin, then bake in the oven until slightly risen and crusty looking: 25 minutes. (A skewer inserted into the centre will not come out clean because the brownies will be moist and slightly runny inside.)

LAVENDER HONEY ICE CREAM

Lavender flowers give this ice cream an unusual, almost peppery flavour that I find very enjoyable in contrast with the honey. Intensely flavoured Provençal lavender honey can be used instead of clear honey and lavender flowers; in this case, omit step 1. Serves 4.

INGREDIENTS

300ml (½ pint) single cream
6 heads of lavender flowers, plus extra to garnish
4 egg yolks
30g (1oz) caster sugar
2 tbsps clear honey
300ml (½ pint) double cream

PREPARATION

1 Put the single cream into a saucepan with the 6 lavender flowers and bring to the boil. Remove from the heat, cover and set aside. This allows the cream to absorb the flavour of the lavender flowers.
2 Whisk the egg yolks and sugar in a bowl until they become creamy and pale: 2–3 minutes.
3 Reheat the cream to boiling point, then pour it through a sieve on to the egg yolks and sugar and stir well to combine.
4 Pour the mixture back into the saucepan and stir it over a low heat until it just thickens and thinly coats the back of a spoon: 2–3 minutes. Be sure to heat it gently to avoid it curdling. Stir in the honey and set the mixture aside to cool.
5 Whip the double cream until it forms soft peaks and fold into the lavender mixture. Pour into a bowl that fits the freezer. Freeze until it begins to solidify around the edges: 15–30 minutes.
6 Take out the partially frozen mixture and whisk it well. Return to the freezer for 15–30 minutes, then whisk again. Repeat until the ice cream is too thick to whisk, then leave it to freeze completely.
7 About 20 minutes before serving, take the ice cream out of the freezer and allow it to soften at room temperature. Serve it in scoops, decorated with lavender flowers.

AMARETTO PARFAIT WITH RASPBERRY COULIS

A parfait is a very rich ice cream that does not need stirring during the freezing process and is soft enough to serve straight from the freezer. You need an electric whisk to make this recipe. Serves 4 to 6.

INGREDIENTS

6 egg yolks
150g (5oz) caster sugar
60ml (4 tbsps) amaretto liqueur
125g (4oz) flaked almonds, toasted and cooled
600ml (1 pint) double cream
THE COULIS
500g (1lb) fresh or frozen raspberries
2 tbsps caster sugar
30ml (2 tbsps) water

PREPARATION

1 Put the egg yolks into a large bowl and whisk until thick and pale.
2 Put the sugar into a small saucepan with 60ml (4 tbsps) of water and heat gently until the sugar has melted. Then raise the heat and let the syrup boil until a drop is thick enough to form a thread when pulled: 1–2 minutes. Be sure not to go past this stage or the syrup will become too hard.
3 Pour the syrup on to the egg yolks, whisking all the time. Continue to whisk until the mixture is very thick and has cooled a little: about 5 minutes.
4 Stir in the amaretto and most of the almonds (reserving a few for decoration). Whip the cream until it forms soft peaks and fold that in too.
5 Turn the parfait into a 1.2-litre (2-pint) bombe mould, loaf tin or other suitable container and freeze until solid.
6 While the parfait is freezing, make the coulis. Put the raspberries into a blender and purée, then sieve them into a saucepan. Alternatively, press them through a sieve directly into the saucepan. Add the sugar and water, place over a moderate heat and bring to the boil. Boil for 1 minute (this makes the coulis clear and glossy). Remove from the heat and allow to cool.
7 To serve the parfait, loosen the sides and turn it out on to a plate, or serve it from the container in scoops. Pour a little of the raspberry coulis over and around each serving and scatter with the reserved almonds.

ROSE SORBET

One of my favourite desserts, this fragrant pink sorbet is best made from the deepest red, most heavily perfumed roses you can find but I have also made it successfully from less than perfect roses. Illustrated on page 129. Serves 4.

INGREDIENTS

petals from 4 large, fragrant, red roses
250g (8oz) caster sugar
300ml (½ pint) water
1 lemon
rose petals to decorate

PREPARATION

1 Put the rose petals, sugar and water into a saucepan and heat gently to dissolve the sugar by the time the mixture boils. Boil for 5 minutes, then remove from the heat and leave to cool.
2 Strain the rose petal mixture through a sieve into a bowl. Squeeze the lemon and add its juice to the mixture in the bowl.
3 Transfer the sorbet mixture to a polythene container and freeze, uncovered, stirring often to help break up crystals of ice. Alternatively, freeze until solid without stirring – for about 6 hours or overnight – then cut it into small chunks and put in a food processor or blender. Blend for a minute or two until the sorbet is soft and fluffy, then return it to the container and freeze again.
4 Serve in scoops, straight from the freezer, and decorate with rose petals.

PASSIONFRUIT & LIME SORBET

This sorbet is easy to make and has a wonderful flavour. I like it with the seeds of the passionfruit left in because they give the sorbet a crunchy texture and a pretty speckled appearance, but you can sieve the mixture to remove them if preferred. Serves 4.

INGREDIENTS

250g (8oz) caster sugar
300ml (½ pint) water
12 passionfruit, halved
1 lime

PREPARATION

1 Dissolve the sugar in the water in a saucepan over a low heat, then raise the heat, bring to the boil and cook until the mixture thickens into a syrup: 3–4 minutes. Remove from the heat and set aside to cool completely.

2 Scoop the pulp and seeds from the passionfruit and add to the syrup, passing through a nylon sieve first to remove the seeds if preferred.
3 Pare long thin shreds of peel from the lime and add most of them to the sorbet mixture, reserving some for decoration. Wrap the reserved shreds of peel in clingfilm to prevent them from drying out. Squeeze the lime and add the juice to the mixture.
4 Transfer the sorbet mixture to a polythene container and freeze, uncovered, stirring often to help break up crystals of ice. Alternatively, freeze until solid without stirring – for about 6 hours or overnight – then cut it into small chunks and put in a food processor or blender. Blend for a minute or two until the sorbet is soft and fluffy, then return to the container and freeze again.
5 Serve in scoops, straight from the freezer, decorated with shreds of lime peel.

TROPICAL FRUIT SALAD

One of the prettiest and healthiest puddings of all, this can be made from any colourful, exotic fruits that are available. The fruit should be ripe. You may need to buy it a day or two in advance to allow time for it to ripen. Serve the salad with Rose sorbet or Passionfruit and lime sorbet (this page), thick yogurt, crème fraîche, or simply on its own. Illustrated on page 128. Serves 6.

INGREDIENTS

4–6 ripe figs
2 starfruit
1 wedge of watermelon
1 large mango
1 small pawpaw
1 pomegranate

PREPARATION

1 Cut each fig into eight segments. Thinly slice the starfruit. Peel the wedge of watermelon and cut the flesh into long thin slices.
2 Make two cuts down the length of the mango, each about 5mm (1.4in) from the stalk, going right through the fruit so that the two halves fall away (leaving a middle section that consists of the large flat stone). Remove the skin from the two halves and cut the flesh into long thin slices.
3 Cut the pawpaw in half, scoop out the shiny black seeds, remove the peel and cut the flesh into long thin slices.
4 Halve the pomegranate and scoop out the seeds, removing any fibrous membrane.
5 Arrange the fruit on a plate and scatter the pomegranate seeds over the top. Serve at once.

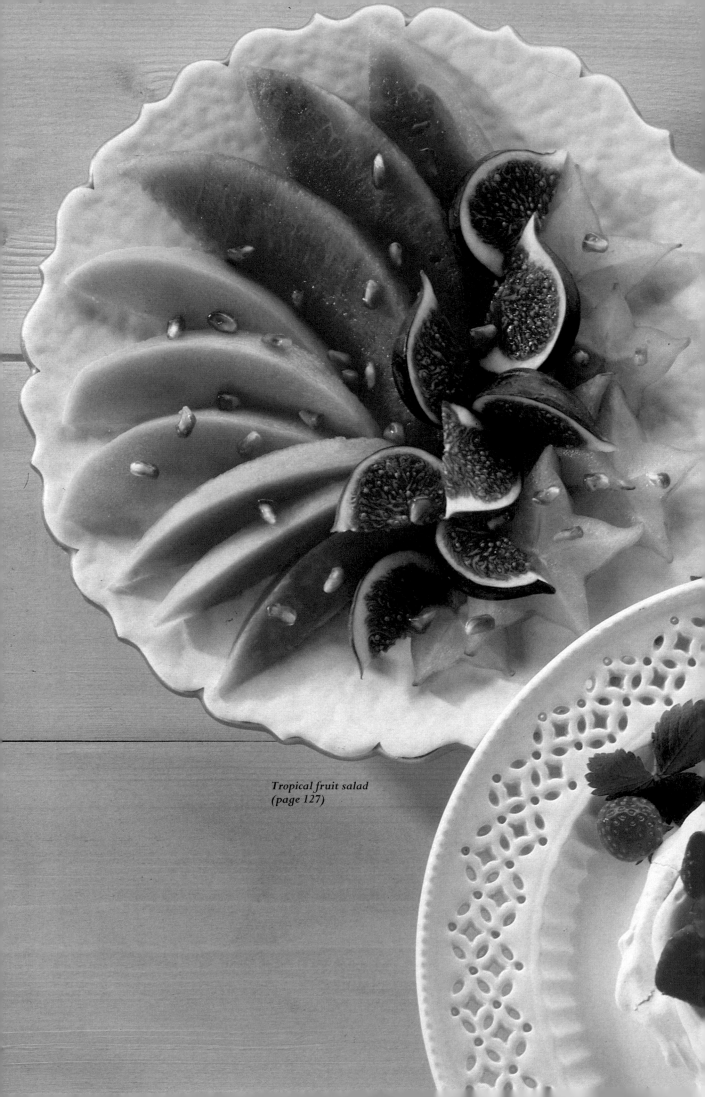

Tropical fruit salad
(page 127)

Rose sorbet
(page 127)

Strawberry pavlova
(page 130)

STRAWBERRY PAVLOVAS

The meringue for these pavlovas is baked at a very low temperature to give it a lovely marshmallowy centre with a crisp outside. Although pavlova is often made as one large meringue, individual portions are also successful; this recipe makes six. Other pretty, soft fruit may be used instead of the strawberries. Illustrated on pages 128−9. Serves 6.

INGREDIENTS

3 egg whites
175g (6oz) caster sugar
1 tsp vanilla extract
1 tsp cornflour
1 tsp white wine vinegar
300ml (½ pint) double cream
250−350g (8−12oz) small ripe strawberries, hulled (leaves reserved to garnish)

PREPARATION

1 Preheat the oven to 130°C/250°F/gas ½. Line a large baking sheet with nonstick paper.
2 Whisk the egg whites in a large greasefree bowl until stiff but not so dry that you can slice them.
3 Sieve the sugar and add it to the egg whites, a heaped tablespoon at a time, whisking well after each addition so the meringue is stiff and glossy.
4 Add the vanilla extract, cornflour and vinegar, and fold in with a large metal spoon.
5 Place the meringue in six mounds on the baking sheet, leaving space around each one. Spread each mound into a circle, first making the centre flat and then fluffing up the sides with a palette knife.
6 Bake until dry and crisp on the outside and still slightly soft in the centre: 1−1½ hours. Leave to cool, then peel them off the paper.

The meringues will keep, in foil or in an airtight container, for up to 1 week in a dry place.

7 Place the meringues on individual plates or in a serving dish. Whip the cream until thick and spoon a little into the centre of each pavlova.
8 Halve most of the strawberries and arrange them over the cream. Decorate the plate with leaves and whole strawberries. Serve at once, or store in the refrigerator for up to two hours.

STRAWBERRY CHEESECAKE

A party piece, this luscious cheesecake has a delectable strawberry topping. It is best made a day ahead, with the topping, which can be varied according to the fruit in season, added later. Serves 8.

INGREDIENTS

90g (3oz) semi-sweet wholewheat biscuits
45g (1½oz) butter
30g (1oz) granulated sugar
500g (1lb) ricotta cheese
175g (6oz) caster sugar
150ml (5fl oz) double cream
3 free-range eggs, separated
juice and finely grated rind of 1 lemon
1 tsp vanilla extract
500g (1lb) small ripe strawberries, hulled
250g (8oz) redcurrant jelly

PREPARATION

1 Preheat the oven to 150°C/300°F/gas 2. Line the base and sides of a 20cm (8in) springclip tin with nonstick paper.
2 On the worktop, run a rolling pin over the biscuits to crush them. Melt the butter in a small saucepan, add the crumbled biscuits and the sugar, stir well to combine and spoon into the prepared tin. Press down firmly using the base of a jar. Set aside while you prepare the cheesecake mixture.
3 Put the ricotta cheese into a large bowl, break it up with a fork, then add the caster sugar, cream, egg yolks, lemon juice and rind and vanilla extract. Beat until the consistency is smooth.
4 Whisk the egg whites in another greasefree bowl until they are stiff but not so dry that you can slice them. Gently fold into the cheesecake mixture using a metal spoon. Pour over the biscuit base in the tin.
5 Bake until the cheesecake is set and a skewer inserted into the centre comes out clean: about 1½ hours. Turn the oven off but leave the cake inside to cool down gently. (Don't worry about cracks in the cake; these largely disappear as the cake cools further and shrinks.)
6 Remove the cheesecake from the oven after an hour or so, cool completely then chill in the refrigerator for 2−3 hours.
7 Arrange the strawberries on top. If they are small they can be used whole, with their points upwards and their stalk ends trimmed so they stand level; if large cut them in half. Melt the redcurrant jelly in a saucepan and spoon over the strawberries to make a thick shiny glaze. Leave until the jelly has cooled and set, then serve.

LEMON TART

Crisp pastry contrasts with cool, tangy lemon to make a refreshing dessert. I like it just as it is, although you could serve cream or crème fraîche with it. Serves 4.

INGREDIENTS

WHITE SHORTCRUST PASTRY
125g (4oz) plain white flour
75g (2½oz) butter, cut into small pieces
THE FILLING
2 large lemons
150g (5oz) caster sugar
2 free-range eggs
150ml (5fl oz) double cream
lemon strips (page 145) to decorate, optional

PREPARATION

1 Preheat the oven to 200°C/400°F/gas 6.
2 Sift the flour into a large bowl or the bowl of a food processor and add the butter. Rub the butter into the flour with your fingertips or work briefly in the food processor until a dough has just formed. Add a little cold water – perhaps a teaspoonful – to make the dough hold together.
3 Turn the dough out on to a lightly floured surface and roll to fit a 20cm (8in) shallow, loose-bottomed flan tin. Slide the pastry off the board and on to the tin. Press it in place, trim it (reserve trimmings) and prick the base (see page 151).
4 Bake the flan case until it is crisp, firm to the touch and turning golden brown: about 15 minutes. Remove and set aside. Turn the oven setting down to 130°C/250°F/gas ½.
5 Make the lemon filling. Finely grate the rind of the lemons into a bowl. Squeeze the lemon juice and add to the bowl. Add the sugar and eggs and whisk to combine. Pour in the cream and whisk again until the consistency is smooth.
6 Fill in any cracks in the pastry case with pastry trimmings, then pour in the lemon mixture and bake the tart in the cool oven until the filling has set and feels firm to a light touch in the middle: about 40 minutes.
7 Take the tart out of the oven and allow it to cool, then chill it in the refrigerator to firm up the lemon custard. Remove it from the tin, place on a serving plate and decorate, if desired, sprinkling lemon strips over the top. Serve chilled.

BLUEBERRY PIE

This double-crust pie can be made with different fruit or with mixtures of fruit. Serve it with Vanilla ice cream (page 124), thick yogurt or crème fraîche. Serves 4.

INGREDIENTS

RICH WHITE SHORTCRUST PASTRY
300g (10oz) plain white flour
175g (6oz) butter, cut into small pieces
30g (1oz) icing sugar
1 egg yolk
THE FILLING
750g (1½lb) blueberries
125g (4oz) caster sugar
2 tbsps cornflour
1 tbsp lemon juice
milk, to glaze
caster sugar, to sprinkle

PREPARATION

1 Preheat the oven to 190°C/375°F/gas 5.
2 Sift the flour into a large bowl or the bowl of a food processor and add the butter, icing sugar and egg yolk. Rub the ingredients together with your fingertips or work briefly in the food processor until a dough has just formed.
3 Turn the dough out on to a lightly floured surface and divide into two pieces, one slightly larger than the other, and knead each one into a smooth round. Wrap in clingfilm and chill in the refrigerator for a few minutes.
4 Place the blueberries, sugar, cornflour and lemon juice in a bowl and mix to combine well.
5 Roll out the smaller piece of pastry on a floured board to fit a 25cm (10in) pie plate or shallow flan dish. Line the plate or dish with the pastry. Pile the blueberry mixture into the dish, leaving a clear 1cm (½in) border all round if you are using a pie plate. Brush the edges with cold water.
6 Roll out the rest of the pastry and place over the fruit. Press the pastry edges together and trim. Flute and scallop the pie rim as shown on page 151. Use a skewer to make two or three steam holes in the centre, then decorate the pie with pastry trimmings.
7 Brush the pie with a little milk, sprinkle with caster sugar, and bake until golden brown: 30 minutes. Serve warm.

JEWELLED FRUIT FLAN

*Use any colourful fruits you like for this flan, but make
sure they are completely ripe. This recipe makes one
large flan or four individual ones. Serves 4.*

INGREDIENTS

butter to grease the baking sheet
250g (8oz) homemade quick flaky pastry
(page 150) or frozen puff pastry
1 free-range egg, beaten
6 tbsps apricot jam
15ml (1 tbsp) lemon juice
100g (3½oz) blueberries
12 strawberries, hulled
2 kiwi fruit, peeled, halved lengthways
and thickly sliced
3 ripe figs, quartered
100g (3½oz) redcurrants
8 Cape gooseberries (physalis), papery sepals pulled back

PREPARATION

1 Preheat the oven to 220°C/425°F/gas 7.
Lightly grease a baking sheet with butter.
2 Roll out the pastry on a floured board and cut
out one square of 25 x 25cm (10 x 10in) or four
of 12.5 x 12.5cm (5 x 5in). Place the square(s) on
the baking sheet and brush the edges with water.
3 Cut the remaining pastry into long thin strips
about 1.5cm (¾in) wide and place them around
the edges to make a single-layer border. Decorate
the border by pressing the back of a knife into it in
a pattern, then "flake" the sides by cutting into
them horizontally, again with the back of the
knife, to encourage the pastry to rise in flakes.
Brush the top of the border with the beaten egg,
being careful not to get any egg on the sides.
4 Bake the pastry case(s) until golden brown and
risen: about 20 minutes. Remove from the oven
and leave on a wire rack to cool.
5 Put the jam into a small saucepan with the
lemon juice and melt over a gentle heat, then
transfer to a small bowl, sieving to remove any
lumps of apricot. Brush a little of this glaze over
the base of the pastry case(s).
6 Arrange the fruit in the pastry case, piled
generously high. Place strawberries with the
pointed end upwards, and any cut fruit with the
cut side downwards. Follow the pattern here, or
make a different pattern, from diagonal lines or
straight lines, for example, or with the fruit
radiating out from the centre.
7 Reheat the remaining glaze and spoon it over
the fruit to cover it thickly. Allow the glaze to
cool and gel, then serve.

Blueberries

Lemon
juice

Apricot jam

Beaten egg

Flaky pastry

Strawberries

Kiwi fruit

Figs

Redcurrants

Cape gooseberries

MENU PLANNING

Menu planning really begins in the shop or market, where you can buy the fresh ingredients and then plan a menu around them. Balance rich dishes with simple ones, making sure that colours and textures are varied, and try not to repeat a key ingredient. If possible, choose crockery that complements the food. Most of all, a menu *you* like is the one your guests are most likely to enjoy.

•

BRUNCHES & LIGHT LUNCHES

These are easy, informal menus, suitable for lunch or brunch.
A fruit juice, or even Buck's fizz, makes a good apéritif, and you could also serve a fruit salad as a refreshing first course.
Mix and match between the menus to cook for a large group of people or to introduce more variety.

BRUNCH PARTY

Warm pasta salad with tomato and basil **or**
*Warm pasta salad with grilled pepper and rocket
(page 56)*

•

Vegetable frittata (page 98) **or**
Four-cheese soufflé (page 26)

Mixed leaf salad with flowers and herbs (page 52)

Light bread rolls (page 103), served warm

•

Blueberry pie (page 131)

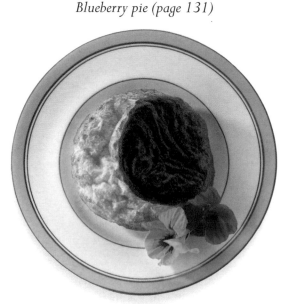

Four-cheese soufflé

LUNCH PARTY

*Twice-baked mushroom or goat's cheese and
thyme soufflés (page 93)*

•

Vegetable paella (page 113) **or**
Porcini risotto (page 114)

*Chicory, watercress, fennel, red onion
and orange salad (page 48)*

•

Strawberry cheesecake (page 130)

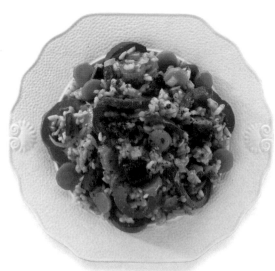

Vegetable paella

INFORMAL SUPPER PARTIES

It's fun to plan an informal supper around a theme, as I've done here. Other possible themes are fondue, which makes a good main dish for 2 to 6 people, or pizza, which can be served do-it-yourself style with lots of toppings to choose from. To feed a crowd, you may want to serve several main courses at once: when cooking pasta, this means using several large saucepans at once and preparing the sauces ahead of time.

PASTA SUPPER

Vegetables à la grecque (page 60) **or**
Insalata tricolore (page 51)

•

Farfalle with broccoli cream sauce (page 88) **or**
Rigatoni with tomato, aubergine and red peppers (page 91)

Rocket salad with flakes of Parmesan (page 53)

•

Selection of ice creams (pages 124 and 126) **or**
Fresh fruit

INDIAN SUPPER

Spiced vegetable triangles (page 110) **or**
Mustard seed crêpes with spiced vegetable filling (page 79)

•

Cashew nut korma (page 70)

Bombay potatoes (page 86)

Spiced okra (page 86) **or**
Green beans with cumin (page 83)

Spinach dal (page 117)

Spiced rice (page 115)

•

Rose sorbet (page 127) **or**
Tropical fruit salad (page 127)

Rigatoni with tomato, aubergine and red peppers

Cashew nut korma

SIMPLE MEALS

The first menu is based around a choice of stir-fries; these versatile dishes can be put together in a few minutes and the meal can be rounded off with fresh fruit, yogurt or a bought ice cream (unless you have one in the freezer). The second menu requires advance preparation and slow cooking, but is perfect for feeding a crowd, especially when you don't know what time everyone is going to arrive.

QUICK MEAL

Thai-style stir-fry vegetables (page 32)
with boiled rice **or**
Summer stir-fry with toasted almonds (page 72)
with boiled rice

•

Fresh fruit, yogurt or biscuits and cheese

PREPARE-AHEAD DINNER

Potato and leek soup (page 46)

Garlic or herb bread (page 47)

•

Spinach, tomato and mozzarella lasagne (page 89)

Mixed salad leaves

•

Jewelled fruit flan (page 132)

Jewelled fruit flan

QUICK & EASY IDEAS

These ideas are for quick everyday meals when you have very little time; I've given a choice of straightforward one-course meals and simple accompaniments with the assumption that you'll serve a labour-free dessert such as fresh seasonal fruit or good cheese. Dress salad leaves in 3 parts olive oil to 1 part balsamic vinegar, with salt and freshly ground black pepper added to taste.

Fresh herb omelette

—— 1 ——
Fresh herb omelette (page 14)

Mixed salad leaves

—— 2 ——
Insalata tricolore (page 51)

Warm pasta salad (chosen from page 56)

—— 3 ——
Deep-fried Brie with apricot sauce (page 97)

Mixed salad leaves

Crusty bread

—— 4 ——
Feuille de chêne, avocado and roasted cashew nuts (page 50)

Crusty bread

Assorted cheeses

—— 5 ——
Vegetarian salade niçoise (page 53)

Baguette

—— 6 ——
Roasted root vegetables (page 75)

Quick herb sauce (page 123)

Crusty bread

—— 7 ——
Spinach dal (page 117)

Sliced tomatoes and onions

Poppadums and mango chutney

—— 8 ——
Roasted Mediterranean vegetables (page 75)

Olives

Ciabatta bread

Mixed salad leaves

—— 9 ——
Vegetable frittata (page 98)

Fresh watercress

Vegetable frittata

PARTIES

The recipe suggestions are for two different sorts of party: a drinks party where you serve finger food along with the liquid refreshments; and a buffet party where guests help themselves to more substantial food. In both cases, colour and contrast of dishes are important. To work out quantities, start from first principles: decide how many slices or portions one guest might have, then multiply by the number of guests.

DRINKS PARTY

Goat's cheese dip (page 58) with crudités

Guacamole (page 59) with crudités

•

Assorted tiny flans and tartlets (chosen from page 105)

Assorted filo parcels (chosen from pages 109–10)

Crostini with spreads (page 47)

Baby aubergines stuffed with mushrooms and nuts (page 64)

Cream cheese mushrooms (page 65)

•

Tropical fruit salad (page 127) served in small pieces on cocktail sticks

BUFFET PARTY

A trio of dips: cucumber and mint dip, curried cashew nut dip and mushroom dip (pages 58–9) with melba toast (page 47) or crudités

•

Tomato, courgette, red pepper and basil terrine (page 10)

Spinach roulade with cream cheese and peppers (page 96)

Parmigiana di melanzane (page 74)

New potato salad (page 50)

Rice salad with herbs, avocado and nuts (page 57)

Mixed leaf salad with flowers and herbs (page 52)

White cabbage salad (page 50)

Garlic or herb bread (page 47), served hot

•

Lemon tart (page 131) **or**
Chocolate and ginger roulade (page 125)

Filo flowers and Money bags

Spinach roulade

OUTDOOR EATING

The main constraint when packing a picnic is how well the
food will travel, but it is surprising what you can take in a
carefully packed box or picnic basket. The barbecue menu is
planned around falafel, cooked on a flat sheet or frying
pan over the barbecue, and Mediterranean vegetables, roasted
on the grill. Whether picnic or barbecue, provide plenty of
bread for filling up and mopping up.

PICNIC

Leek and sesame flan

Broccoli and Brie flans (page 28) **or**
Leek and sesame flans (page 105)

Tabbouleh (page 57)

Peppers filled with grilled vegetables (page 65)

Vegetarian salade niçoise (page 53)

•

Double-chocolate brownies (page 125) **or**
Fresh fruit

BARBECUE

Gazpacho (page 45)

•

Falafel (page 117) with fresh or sundried
tomato sauce (page 121)

Roasted Mediterranean vegetables (page 75)

Green leaves with goat's cheese and walnuts
(page 52) **or**
Rocket salad with flakes of Parmesan (page 53)

Potatoes or sweetcorn, part-cooked, wrapped in foil
and buried in the fire embers

•

Blueberry pie (page 131) **or**
Lemon tart (page 131)

Peppers filled with grilled vegetables

Gazpacho

SPECIAL DINNERS

These are formal vegetarian meals for special events and celebrations.
The meals are impressive, but not difficult. Many of the dishes, such
as the roulade, can be made in advance and require only a little
last-minute attention. Serving a first course that can be prepared in
advance and an easy but luxurious dessert, as these menus suggest,
also makes life easier. If you are nervous, have a trial run of the menu
on an unstressful occasion to build up confidence. Then, on the
special day, relax and enjoy the party along with everyone else.

WINTER DINNER PARTY

Blue cheese, leek and watercress terrine (page 69)
Red wine sauce (page 121)

•

Gruyère gougère (page 108)

Gratin dauphinois (page 80)

Spinach with nutmeg (page 83)

•

Strawberry pavlovas (page 130) **or**
Passionfruit and lime sorbet (page 127)

SUMMER DINNER PARTY

Cucumber and tarragon soup (page 46), iced **or**
Tomato-filled artichoke (page 22)

•

Gruyère and herb roulade with asparagus
(page 34)

Mixed leaf salad with flowers and herbs (page 52)

Carrot and courgette ribbons with pesto (page 82)

New potatoes

•

Strawberry cheesecake (page 130) **or**
Rose sorbet (page 127)

Strawberry pavlova

CHRISTMAS DINNERS

Christmas is a wonderful opportunity to show how delicious
vegetarian food can be. I like to serve a "showy" main course, such
as the cashew nut and tomato pâté en croûte, the vegetable strudel
or a colourful roulade, because it makes a good focal point.
Alongside these serve vegetables in season and, if you wish,
traditional trimmings such as cranberry sauce. Have a simple but
delicious first course, and a luxurious pudding at the end,
and you'll have a meal to remember.

CHRISTMAS DINNER 1

*Chicory, watercress, fennel, red onion
and orange salad (page 48)* **or**
*Twice-baked goat's cheese and thyme soufflés
(page 93)*

•

Cashew nut and tomato pâté en croûte (page 106) **or**
Vegetable strudel (page 16)

Red wine sauce (page 121)

Fantail roast potatoes (page 81)

Buttered leeks with parsley (page 83)

Celeriac purée (page 83)

•

Chocolate and ginger roulade (page 125) **or**
*Vanilla-poached pears with ice cream
and chocolate sauce (page 124)*

CHRISTMAS DINNER 2

Creamy leek and tarragon crêpes (page 38) **or**
Pumpkin, broccoli and leek terrine (page 69)

•

*Cheddar and herb roulade with
mushrooms (page 94)*

Red wine sauce (page 121)

Spiced red cabbage and apple (page 87)

Julienne of kohlrabi (page 82) **or**
Roasted root vegetables (page 75)

•

Amaretto parfait with raspberry coulis (page 126) **or**
Tropical fruit salad (page 127)

Cashew nut and tomato pâté en croûte

Creamy leek and tarragon crêpes

TECHNIQUES

*Part of the pleasure of cooking is handling
fresh fruit and vegetables, cracking eggs, choosing
herbs and spices: all part of the process of
transforming basic ingredients into delicious meals.
This section contains useful kitchen information,
such as how to prepare artichokes, make béchamel
sauce and crêpe batter, cook rice and bake the
perfect flan case. It also lists the essential
items for the well-stocked storecupboard, and
gives advice on what kitchen equipment
is indispensable.*

PREPARING VEGETABLES

A few simple techniques go a long way towards making cookery pleasurable. With garlic, for example, I pull off the papery skin and then roughly chop the flesh with a sharp knife, or crush it using the blunt side of a knife. I peel tomatoes by covering them with hot water, but I rarely deseed them. The slightly indigestible skin of red peppers can be removed by grilling. The following pages show my favourite methods of preparing and cooking vegetables and – because looks are also important – the easy garnishes I use.

PEELING A TOMATO

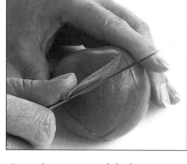

Cover the tomato with boiling water. After 10 seconds pierce the skin with the point of a knife. If the skin splits, drain the tomato and peel it; if not, leave it for a few seconds longer.

PEELING A PEPPER

Quarter the pepper. Place under a hot grill, shiny side up, until the skin blisters and turns black. Allow to cool. Tear off the papery skin, and remove and discard the stalk and seeds.

CHOPPING FRESH HERBS

Wash fresh herbs well and dry them in a salad spinner or on kitchen paper. Remove large stalks from herbs such as flat-leaf parsley, then chop the herb with a knife. Hold the point down with one hand while you rock the handle with the other, sweeping back and forth over the herb until it is finely chopped.

GARNISHES

Garnishing a dish makes it special – and the simpler the garnish the better. Best of all is to make creative use of ingredients from the recipe so you have a garnish that is appropriate.

CARROT KNOT
Cut a long sliver of carrot, tie it into a loose knot and tuck the ends in.

LEMON STRIP
Take a thin piece of peel from a lemon, remove any pith, and cut the peel into delicate strips, as fine as you like.

SPRING ONION TASSELS
Slice into one or both ends, turning the onion around as you cut through it. Place in iced water so the cut ends curl.

MAKING VEGETABLE STICKS AND DICE

This is a useful and attractive way to cut many vegetables, not just carrots. It may be easier to do if you square off unevenly shaped vegetables first; you can use the trimmings when making stock.

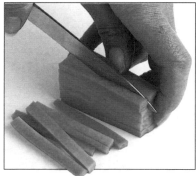

1 Cut the vegetable into parallel slices about 5mm (¼in) wide. If you want to make fine strips (juliennes), cut the slices much more thinly.

2 Stack the slices and cut down through them to make sticks. Cut more finely to make julienne strips.

3 Cut across the sticks to make them into small dice, for use in soups, sauces and fillings.

PREPARING VEGETABLES

CHOPPING AN ONION

1 Trim the onion, removing the root, and peel off the papery skin. Wash the onion, then cut it in half from the stalk end to the root end.

2 Cut the onion along its markings from root end to tip, making the cuts close or further apart depending on how finely chopped the onion needs to be.

3 Turn the onion and slice it again, so that the cuts are at right angles to the first ones.

DESEEDING CHILLIES

There are many different varieties of chilli, varying greatly in hotness. They are notoriously difficult to identify, but as a general rule the smaller the chilli, the hotter the flavour. If in doubt, seek advice, or better still, taste – cautiously!

1 Halve the chilli, then remove the seeds, stalk and inner white part. Be very careful not to touch your face or get juice in your eyes as chilli can burn.

2 Rinse the chilli under the tap. Cut lengthways into strips, then crossways into small pieces. Wash your hands after handling chillies.

ARTICHOKES: PREPARING THE RAW BASE

STUFFING (COOKED)

1 Cut off the top and stalk of the uncooked artichoke, then cut away the leaves, leaving the base. Squeeze with lemon juice to preserve its colour.

2 Scoop out the tiny central leaves and fluffy "choke". Rinse the base. Cook in boiling water until just tender and use as described in the recipe.

1 After boiling, press back the outer leaves, discard the central leaf cluster and scrape away the "choke". Stuff as described in the recipe.

CLEANING LEEKS

1 Cut off the root and trim the green leaves, cutting off damaged or very coarse ones.

2 Slit the leek from the top to about halfway down; rinse carefully under the cold tap, opening up the layers and making sure all the grit is washed away.

PREPARING GARLIC

Twist the clove of garlic between finger and thumb of each hand to loosen the skin. Remove the skin and chop or crush the flesh using a sharp knife. To crush the flesh, press down all over it with the blunt side of a knife tip. For an extra smooth result, make a paste by rubbing salt into the flesh.

SALAD LEAVES

Store salad leaves unwashed in the bottom of the refrigerator, then wash thoroughly and dry before use. To dry, use a salad spinner, or drain in a colander and then dry on kitchen paper.

COOKING METHODS

HALF-BOIL, HALF-STEAM METHOD

For up to 750g (1½lb) green vegetables, pour 1cm (⅓in) of boiling water into a pan. Put in the vegetables, cut up well, bring back to the boil, cover and half-boil, half-steam for a few minutes until tender.

STIR-FRYING

A stainless steel wok is best for this technique, though a large frying pan can be used. Prepare the vegetables in advance, then heat a tablespoon of oil, such as groundnut, until smoking hot. Add the vegetables and stir vigorously while they fry until they are heated through but still crisp: a few minutes.

BAIN-MARIE

When cooking a delicate dish, such as an egg-set terrine, stand the baking dish in a large tin of very hot water and place in the oven with the temperature on low. This method works on the hob, too: set a bowl over a pan of simmering water to achieve the gentle heat required for making hollandaise sauce, melting chocolate or keeping a dish of food warm.

STEAMING

Steaming is an excellent way of cooking small to medium-sized amounts of vegetables – with the exception of leafy green vegetables, which I think are best half-boiled, half-steamed (see left). A stainless steel steamer set over a saucepan is ideal: you can cook one vegetable in the steamer while another is half-boiling, half-steaming in the pan below, saving heat and space.

DEEP-FRYING

To fry a small quantity of food, it is best to use an ordinary saucepan, not a vast deep-frier. For larger quantities you can also use a wok. Fill the pan no more than half-full with oil (less for a wok): both groundnut and soya oils are suitable. The oil needs to be hot: 180°C/350°F. Use a kitchen thermometer, or dip the handle of a wooden spoon or a wooden chopstick into the oil – bubbles will instantly form around the spoon handle or chopstick if the oil is hot enough. Make sure the food is dry when you put it in to prevent splattering, retrieve it after cooking using a slotted spoon, and drain it well on crumpled kitchen paper. Ideally, replace oil after using it twice.

EGGS & MILK

Eggs and milk are useful and effective ingredients. For instance, the air whisked into egg whites makes soufflés rise, while egg yolks make custards and terrines set. Milk is the basis for one of the most useful sauces, béchamel, while delicious crêpes and pancakes are made with milk, eggs and flour. And of course, eggs on their own make the classically simple omelette.

BECHAMEL SAUCE

To make 300ml (½ pint) of medium-thick sauce, use:

30g (1oz) butter
30g (1oz) flour
350ml (12fl oz) milk

MAKING THE ROUX

ADDING THE MILK

1 Melt the butter in a saucepan over a moderate heat, then add the flour and stir until the flour is incorporated: 1–2 minutes.

2 Over the heat pour in one-third of the milk and stir well; the mixture will go lumpy, then thick and smooth. Stir in another third of the milk, and then repeat with the final third.

3 Simmer over gentle heat for 7–10 minutes then test the consistency: it should be thick enough to coat a spoon. To thin, stir in milk or cream; to thicken, simmer for a little longer.

FOLDING AN OMELETTE

1 Cook the omelette gently until it begins to set, drawing the edges in with a fork. When underneath is set but the top is still creamy, loosen the edges with a spatula and fold over one-third.

2 Tip the pan and slide the omelette onto a warm plate. As it slides out flip the folded section over again, using the spatula if necessary, so that the omelette is folded in three.

FILLED OMELETTES
This technique is usually used for filled omelettes. Place the filling in the centre before folding in three. Sweet omelettes may be spread with jam before folding.

SEPARATING AN EGG

Make sure the bowl you use is completely free from grease. Crack the egg and then, holding it over the bowl, let the white run into the bowl. Transfer the yolk from one half of the shell to the other to allow more white to run into the bowl. Take care not to get even a speck of egg yolk in with the whites, or they won't whisk.

CREPE BATTER

Makes twelve 15cm (6in) crêpes.

INGREDIENTS

125g (4oz) wholemeal flour
pinch of salt
2 free-range eggs
15ml (1 tbsp) olive oil or melted butter
300ml (½ pint) milk

PREPARATION

FOOD PROCESSOR METHOD: Place all the ingredients in a food proccsssor or blcndcr and blend until smooth.

HAND METHOD: Sift the flour and salt into a bowl. Make a well in the centre and break in the eggs. Add the oil or butter. Stir the mixture with a wire whisk then gradually add the milk, beating the batter until it is smooth.

Tossing pancakes on Shrove Tuesday is a long-standing tradition. Use the crêpe batter recipe above, but make the pancakes much thicker if you want to toss them.

PASTRY

Shortcrust and quick flaky pastry are not nearly as complicated to make as many people think. In fact it's easy and satisfying to make your own, and learning the basics will open up a whole repertoire of dishes. Filo pastry, bought ready-made, is also simple to use and can produce stunning results.

BASIC SHORTCRUST PASTRY

*Makes one 20cm (8in) flan case
or four 10cm (4in) individual flan cases,
or 8 or more tartlets, depending on their size.*

INGREDIENTS

*60g (2oz) wholemeal flour
60g (2oz) plain flour
¼ tsp salt
60g (2oz) butter, cut into pieces
1 egg yolk, optional
20–30ml (1½–2 tbsps) water*

PREPARATION

1 Sift the flours and salt into a large bowl, adding the bran left in the sieve.
2 Add the butter and rub it in with your fingertips or work briefly in a food processor until the mixture resembles breadcrumbs.
3 Add the egg yolk if desired (it gives the pastry an extra light, crisp texture) and enough cold water to make a dough that leaves the edges of the bowl clean. Wrap in clingfilm and chill in the refrigerator for 30 minutes.
4 Preheat the oven to 200°C/400°F/gas 6.
5 Roll the pastry out thinly on a lightly floured board. To make individual flan cases, divide the pastry into four and roll each one out separately. Wholemeal pastry is more fragile than white because of the bran, so do not attempt to lift it. Use the board, as shown above right, to transfer the pastry into the tin.
6 Line and prepare the tin(s) as shown. Press the pastry gently into place, trim off surplus, and prick the base with a fork. To prevent the pastry bubbling up while cooking, bake it blind: line the pastry case with nonstick paper or foil and weigh it down with dried beans.
7 Bake in the centre of the preheated oven for 15 minutes, then remove the beans and paper and bake for a further 10 minutes, or until the pastry is crisp and golden brown.

QUICK FLAKY PASTRY

Makes approximately 300g (10oz)

INGREDIENTS

*175g (6oz) strong white flour
¼ tsp salt
125g (4oz) cold butter
squeeze of lemon juice
small jug of icy water*

PREPARATION

1 Sift the flour and salt into a large bowl and place in the refrigerator or freezer to chill thoroughly: about ½ hour. The colder the ingredients are for this pastry, the better.
2 Grate the butter into the flour, dipping it in flour if it becomes too sticky to grate.
3 Add a squeeze of lemon juice, then, mixing with a fork, stir in enough icy water to make a lumpy dough that just holds together and leaves the sides of the bowl clean.
4 Gather the dough up into a ball, wrap it in clingfilm and chill for 30 minutes.
5 Preheat the oven to 200°C/400°F/gas 6.
6 Roll the pastry out thinly on a lightly floured board and use as required.

USING FILO PASTRY

• *Although you can make filo pastry at home, I really don't think it is worth it — some of the supermarket own brands are exceptional. Recipes in this book are based on sheets of filo measuring approximately 320 x 200mm (13 x 8in).*

• *Brush a sheet of filo pastry with butter and place another sheet on top for a deliciously flaky effect. Don't brush if you prefer low-fat pastry.*

• *Filo pastry dries out and becomes brittle on contact with the air, so remove one sheet at a time and keep the rest covered with clingfilm or a damp tea towel until needed.*

MAKING A FLAN CASE

Wholemeal pastry is crumbly, so it helps to transfer it to the tin using the board. My method (see step 4) of "waterproofing" the flan case before adding the filling is unusual, but it helps to avoid soggy bases.

1 Leave the rolled-out pastry on the board, making sure it's not sticking. Hold the board over the far rim of the tin, then slide the pastry off the board into the tin.

2 Gently ease the pastry into the edges of the tin and press lightly but firmly into position.

3 Run a rolling pin over the tin to detach the excess pastry. Prick the base with a fork and line with nonstick paper or foil and beans. Bake until crisp and lightly browned, removing paper and beans after 15 minutes.

4 Heat 30ml (2 tbsps) vegetable oil in a small pan. As soon as the flan comes out of the oven, spoon the hot oil over the hot pastry: it will sizzle, frying the surface of the pastry and "waterproofing" it.

PIE PREPARATION

Use a pie dish, and heap up the filling in the centre to give the pie an attractive domed shape. Make sure the filling has completely cooled before you cover it, or the flaky pastry may start to melt.

1 To make the edge of the pie rise in flakes, cut into it with the back of a knife. Then scallop the pie by going around the edge with your finger and the back of a knife as shown.

2 Cut diamond shapes from a strip of leftover pastry, and score with the back of the knife to make "leaf veins". Arrange on top of the pie, brushing with water or milk to seal.

3 To glaze, brush the pie with milk or beaten egg mixed with ½tsp salt (the salt helps to make the glaze shiny). Cut a vent for the steam to escape.

You can decorate the pie with a variety of shapes. Little cocktail cutters are useful for hearts, stars and other shapes.

GRAINS, PULSES & SPICES

Rice, millet and other grains, dried beans, lentils, nuts and seeds are all wonderfully nutritious, providing a healthy source of protein in the vegetarian diet. The many varieties of grain require fairly similar preparation, so once the principles are understood there is room to experiment. Nuts and seeds can be prepared, too: toasted to enhance their flavour or ground to alter their texture.

COOKING RICE

Many varieties of rice are widely available. My staple is long-grain brown rice, but I also like long-grain white rice and I love the delicate fragrance of basmati rice, both brown and white. For risottos I use Italian arborio rice: other varieties don't give the same creamy result. Various types of glutinous short-grain or "sticky" rice, whose grains cling together, are also available. Wild rice (not really a grain but a grass) is delicious mixed with other kinds of rice.

ABSORPTION METHOD

A useful method for the busy cook. Allow 1 measure of rice to 2 of water or 250g (8oz) to 600ml (1 pint). Put in a pan and bring to the boil. Cover tightly, turn the heat down to low and cook until the rice is tender and the water absorbed (see times opposite). Remove from the heat and keep covered for a further 5 – 10 minutes. Fluff up the rice with a fork.

DRAINING METHOD

Bring 3 litres (5 pints) of water to the boil in a large saucepan. Add 250g (8oz) rice and stir. Cook until the rice is tender: 12 minutes for long-grain white rice, 20–25 minutes for brown, around 10 for white basmati, 15 for brown. Drain, rinse under hot water, drain again and spoon into a warmed dish with seasoning and, if liked, a little butter.

SHORT-GRAIN RICE

Glutinous short-grain rice is much used in Thai, Chinese and Japanese cooking. Because of its high starch content the grains tend to clump together, instead of being fluffy and separate. This makes it ideal for Eastern dishes, as it is easy to pick up sticky rice with chopsticks. This rice is used for both sweet and savoury dishes. Cook by the absorption method (see above).

RICE COOKING TIMES

These cooking times are for the absorption method of cooking rice and are based on 250g (8oz) rice and 600ml (1 pint) water — allow fractionally less water for basmati rice and fractionally more for brown rice (up to 1¼ pints). You can also add some salt, though rice is a food that I prefer unsalted. Rinse basmati rice before cooking by swirling it in a large bowl of water, then drain. Repeat 2–3 times: this gives a lighter result.

Long-grain white rice 15–20 minutes

Long-grain brown rice 40–45 minutes

White basmati rice 10–15 minutes

Brown basmati rice 15–20 minutes

Glutinous short-grain rice 20 minutes

Wild rice 45 minutes

COUSCOUS AND BULGUR

The easiest way to cook these grains is to put one tablespoon of oil into a large saucepan with 350ml (12fl oz) water and 1½ teaspoons salt. Bring to the boil, then add 250g (8oz) couscous or bulgur. Remove from the heat and leave to swell: 2 minutes for couscous, 10 for bulgur. Add a little butter and heat gently, stirring with a fork, until heated through: about 3 minutes.

PREPARING DRIED BEANS

Cover beans with cold water and soak for 8 – 12 hours. Drain, rinse, then place in pan and cover with their height again in cold water. Boil hard for 10 minutes, then reduce the heat and simmer until tender: 1 – 1½ hours for most beans.

SEEDS AND SPICES

Many seeds make wonderful flavourings. They range from the aromatics, such as sesame and fennel, to the spicy-flavoured, such as cumin, cardamom and coriander, much used in Eastern and Indian cooking.

DRY-FRYING SPICES

To bring out their flavour, crush spices before use, and heat them in a dry pan for a few minutes. Cumin, coriander, fennel and cardamom seeds respond particularly well. Sesame seeds are delicious toasted lightly in a dry pan or under a hot grill, but watch them in case they burn.

Cumin   **Sesame**

PREPARING STAR ANISE

You can use star anise whole, or you can break off the points of the "star" and crush them lightly with your fingers to free the shiny seeds. Use these seeds whole or lightly crushed.

PREPARING CARDAMOM

Bruise cardamom pods in a pestle and mortar then add to spicy dishes; or crush to loosen the outer casings, then remove these and crush the remaining tiny seeds to a powder.

GRATING GINGER

Wash but don't bother to peel the ginger – the peel comes away easily as you grate. To prepare ginger for cooking, use the small holes (but not the very smallest) on a flat grater or box grater .

GROUND SEEDS FOR SPICE

Many seeds used as spices – such as coriander and cumin – can be bought in ground form. Since ground spices quickly lose their aroma, check your storecupboard regularly and throw away those that have lost their fragrance. Buy ground spices in small quantities and use them quickly, or grind the spices yourself to ensure freshness.

TOASTING NUTS AND SEEDS

Spread the nuts or seeds in the grill pan or on a baking sheet. Grill for a few minutes or bake at 180°C/350°F/gas 4 until golden brown. Keep an eye on them; some nuts toast quickly. Use at once or store in an airtight container for a few days.

THE VEGETARIAN PANTRY

Classic vegetarian cookery does not demand strange ingredients that are difficult to obtain: most are widely available. Buy the best quality you can and store them carefully, as described.

Keeping the basics in store means you can always put a simple meal together. To store herbs and spices, I prefer open shelves to cupboards: seeing them gives me inspiration while I work.

THE PANTRY

A cool, dry, airy cupboard is ideal for most non-perishable foods. Keep some of these in stock and you'll save a great deal of time and be able to put together quick meals at short notice. It's best to buy flours, grains and pulses in small quantities and keep them in airtight jars, or wrap in an outer polythene bag once opened.

FRUIT & VEGETABLES
Most fruit and vegetables are best kept in the refrigerator; those for the pantry include dried fruits such as apricots and raisins; citrus fruits, apples and bananas; unripe avocados and mangos (once ripe put them in the refrigerator); onions, garlic and potatoes.

FRESH HERBS
Herbs in pots can be kept on a windowsill until used up.

FLAVOURINGS
All of the following are useful to keep in store:
• Sea salt: I like the light flaky kind that crumbles in your fingers.
• Black peppercorns in a grinder.
• Red and white wine vinegars, rice and balsamic vinegars.
• Soy sauce: good quality, made without colouring or caramel.
• Jar of light tahini or sesame seed paste (stir before use).
• Honeys of different types.
• Dried porcini mushrooms.
• Vegetarian bouillon powder.
• Stem ginger in syrup.

SPICES
Buy in small quantities so that you can use them up while they're fresh and fragrant. I keep mine lined up in alphabetical order on long shelves over my work surface.

OILS
These are the oils I keep in store:
• Light olive oil, perfect for all basic cooking. I also keep a bottle of the best olive oil I can afford, which I use in salads.
• Groundnut oil for deep-frying.
• Toasted sesame oil for fragrant and flavoursome stir-fries.
• Walnut oil for salads – expensive but a treat.

CANNED FOODS
I keep these cans in store:
• Artichoke hearts in brine.
• Whole plum tomatoes in juice.
• Various beans and lentils: whole green lentils, red kidney beans, chickpeas and cannellini beans are all useful.
• Bamboo shoots and straw mushrooms for Chinese-style stir-fries.

PACKET FOODS
These are good to keep at hand but remember that most don't last indefinitely, so they should be sorted regularly. All of the following are essential:
• Various shapes of dried pasta.
• White and wholemeal flour; also cornflour or potato flour.
• Bulgur, couscous and polenta.
• Long-grain and basmati rice, both brown and white; plus arborio rice for risottos.
• Split red lentils.
• Brown sugar; white caster sugar with a vanilla pod buried in it.

USEFUL SPICES

Bay leaves
Cardamom pods
Cayenne pepper **or** chilli powder
Cinnamon powder
Cinnamon sticks
Cloves, whole and ground
Coriander, whole and ground
Cumin, whole and ground
Fennel seeds
Garam masala
Ginger, ground
Mustard powder
Mustard seeds
Nutmeg, whole
Paprika
Saffron
Star anise
Turmeric, ground

THE REFRIGERATOR

I recommend any vegetarian or would-be vegetarian buying a new refrigerator to get the biggest one possible because the refrigerator is such a good place to store fruit and vegetables, and having a capacious one means being able to store enough for up to a week at a time. It is also the place, of course, for dairy foods.

VEGETABLES

All of the following keep best in the refrigerator: all green leafy vegetables, all root vegetables except potatoes and sweet potatoes, green beans, mangetout, fresh mushrooms, courgettes, aubergines, peppers, beansprouts, fresh baby sweetcorn, spring onions, asparagus, leeks, fennel, tomatoes, celery, cucumber, cauliflower, broccoli, and pumpkin once it's been cut.

FRUIT

Once fully ripened, delicate fruits keep longer if stored in the refrigerator: figs, apricots, peaches, pears, mango, pawpaw, star fruit, plums, cherries, and melon once it's been cut.

FRESH HERBS

Packets of fresh herbs go into the refrigerator but bunches of fresh coriander and flat-leaf parsley keep well – and look attractive – standing in a jug of water on a kitchen shelf.

EGGS

Free-range eggs, preferably from a small producer, are the only kind I ever use and I keep them in the refrigerator.

CHEESE

Cheddar, Parmesan and Gruyère are the basics that I always keep, carefully wrapped, in the refrigerator. At other times I may have Brie, a goat's cheese log, Camembert, feta, mozzarella (packed in water), blue cheese, and soft white cheese ranging from low-fat versions to curd cheese, cream cheese (especially the type flavoured with herbs and garlic) and mascarpone. Vegetarian cheeses, that is, made with vegetarian rennet, are often available: if this information is not given on the packet, do ask.

MILK, YOGURT & CREAM

I buy milk, yogurt and cream – single, whipping, double, soured or crème fraîche – in small quantities as and when needed.

FATS

Salted and unsalted butter are my basics. For vegan dishes I use unhydrogenated margarine. I also store creamed coconut to use in curries; it keeps well.

FLAVOURINGS

All of these are useful: fresh ginger, olives, sundried tomatoes and sundried tomato paste, tubes of tomato purée once opened, lemongrass, fresh chillies, mustard including Dijon, capers in salt and creamed horseradish.

THE FREEZER

The freezer is handy for keeping a supply of certain ingredients, such as fruit, vegetables and pastry, and is very useful for emergencies. If I have a big event to cook for, like a family Christmas, I make some dishes in advance and freeze them, but on the whole I prefer to make dishes fresh when they're needed.

FRUIT & VEGETABLES

Sweetcorn, peas, broad beans and leaf spinach; and some frozen raspberries for a treat.

NUTS

If you buy large quantities, keep them in the freezer to stop them going rancid. You can use them straight from the freezer.

PASTRY

Frozen puff and filo pastry are useful. Re-freeze unused filo.

OTHER FOODS

Small portions of frozen cream are useful for when just a little is needed for a sauce or soup. And if I have an abundance of stock I freeze it in small batches.

FOOD TO FREEZE

• *Pastry flan cases, either cooked or ready for cooking.*

• *Crêpes, ready for stuffing or serving with sugar and lemon.*

• *One or two vegetarian savoury dishes that are quick to reheat, such as small twice-baked soufflés, miniature flans and lasagne made in individual portions.*

• *Packets of filo pastry, both unopened and resealed. Wrap the pastry in clingfilm before resealing.*

NOTES ON EQUIPMENT

BAKING TINS

Gradually build up a collection of strong tins: they will last a lifetime if chosen carefully. Most useful are two sizes of 500g (1lb) loaf tin: one 7.5cm (3in) deep, and a shallower one, 5.5cm (2in) deep. A small Swiss roll tin measuring 18 x 28cm (7 x 11in) and a medium-sized one measuring 25 x 35cm (10 x 14in) are also worth having. A strong baking tin with shallow sides is best for roasting vegetables and can double as a baking sheet.

Flan tins of various sizes are useful: I like a 20cm (8in) round one with a removable base for most kinds of flan. For small individual flans, I use 10cm (4in) tins with shallow sides of about 1.5cm (¾in). A dozen tiny barquette tins are perfect for tartlets; for a big batch, remove the pastry cases once cooled and re-use the tins. Also useful are a 20cm (8in) springclip tin, a 20cm (8in) square baking tin and a bun or muffin tin with 12 sections.

FRYING PANS

I don't use anything other than nonstick frying pans. A frying pan measuring about 28cm (11in) across the top is useful for general frying. Ideally you should also have a special omelette pan (with rounded sides) and a crêpe pan (with straight, shallow sides), each measuring about 15cm (6in) across the base. In fact, I use an omelette pan for both.

CASSEROLES & DISHES

Rectangular baking dishes about 5cm (2in) deep, measuring around 19 x 29cm (7½ x 11½in) and 24 x 32cm (9½ x 13in) are essential for such dishes as lasagne (in the larger dish) and gratin dauphinois (the smaller dish). Other useful items are small ramekin dishes and timbale moulds, straight-sided soufflé dishes, a big oval serving dish and ovenproof pizza plates.

SAUCEPANS

Gradually build up a collection of good, strong pans in different sizes. I like good quality stainless steel. I also have a stainless-steel pressure cooker which I use frequently for soup – as it is so quick.

WOK

I use a wok not only for stir-frying but also for deep-frying: the surface area of oil in a wok is greater than the surface area of the same amount of oil in a straight-sided pan. This means using less oil, and so it is not so extravagant to change it often. I use a stainless steel wok, with a heatproof handle.

FOOD PROCESSOR / BLENDER

Although you can cook vegetarian food without one, a food processor opens up a whole new range of possibilities. Buy an easy-to-assemble model that does all the basics – chopping, grating and slicing – so you do not need to spend money on extras. A large-capacity one that will process soups easily is also a good idea. A blender (liquidizer) is useful for soups and purées but is not nearly as versatile as a food processor.

CHOPPING BOARD

This is my most vital piece of equipment, along with my two favourite sharp knives and my potato peeler. I use a thick, strong wooden board not less than 30 x 40cm (12 x 16in); some people prefer firm white plastic. Either type doubles as a pastry board.

GRATER

A box grater that you can stand on the chopping board is just right for grating small quantities of cheese or vegetables. I also use a small hand-held rotary grater with different-sized drums and a small nutmeg grater with a compartment for storing the nutmeg.

KITCHEN SCISSORS

Scissors make quick work of many jobs such as snipping fresh herbs and trimming filo pastry.

KNIVES

The essential knife is a traditional, good quality French chef's knife with a 13cm (5in) blade. Buy an expensive one and it will last for years; hold it first to check the balance before you buy. You'll also need a steel for sharpening the knife. Second most essential in my opinion is a knife with a 13cm (5in) serrated, stainless steel blade.

PESTLE & MORTAR

Not essential, but useful for crushing spices. Choose a heavy ceramic one with a reasonably sized mortar; it works best when the mortar is less than half-full.

POTATO PEELER

A sharp, swivel-bladed potato peeler is an essential piece of equipment; I prefer a peeler with a long, comfortable handle (many are far too short).

ROLLING PIN

An essential item if you make a lot of pastry, although it is possible to improvise with a substitute, such as a wine bottle. I prefer to use a long wooden rolling pin, without handles.

WHISK

For years I put off buying a hand-held electric whisk but when I eventually bought one (in a sale) I couldn't believe how useful it was. Now I consider it one of my most vital pieces of equipment – and it's relatively cheap. Choose a lightweight one with a switch that's easy to operate.

INDEX

ACKNOWLEDGMENTS

Author's appreciation
I would like to thank everyone involved in producing this book for their inspiration, care and attention to detail and for making the whole process such a pleasure. My warmest thanks and appreciation firstly to Christopher Davis and Daphne Razazan for being so enthusiastic from the beginning; and to Rosie Pearson and Carole Ash; to my wonderful editor and art editor, Mari Roberts and Tracey Clarke, with whom I so much enjoyed working; to the photographers Amanda Heywood and Clive Streeter, for taking so much trouble and making the photo sessions so pleasant; to all the talented food stylists, particularly Lyn Rutherford, for preparing the recipes so well for the photographs; to my agent Barbara Levy; to my daughter Claire for tasting and fun, and most especially my husband Robert for support, (more!) tasting, and living with all that writing a book entails.

Dorling Kindersley would like to thank Alexa Stace and Lorna Damms for editorial help; Lyn Rutherford, Kathy Man, Carole Handslip and Jill Eggleton for preparing the food that appears throughout the book; Sarah Ponder for the artworks; Sarah Ereira for the index and Artemi Kyriacou for photographic assistance.